MINIMALIST GARDENING

MINIMALIST GARDENING

DAVID THE GOOD

Minimalist Gardening
David The Good

Published by Good Books.

Cover design by Rutger Leroy Kipling.
Illustrations by Tom Sensible.
Copyright © Good Books 2024.

ISBN: 978-1-955289-14-6

This book or parts thereof may not be reproduced in any form, stored in a retrieval system, or transmitted in any form by any means without prior written permission of the publisher.

Contents

Introduction: Why Minimalism?		i
1	Complexity, Engineers vs. Rastas, and Remembering the Point	1
2	The Wide World of Raised Bed Gardening	39
3	Dejunking Your Garden	59
4	Free Fertilizer	73
5	Watering Made Easy	91
6	You Can Do Everything with a Machete	103
7	Grow the Simple Stuff	107
8	Grapes on Trees and Other Stories	123
9	Gardening Without Money	145
10	Year-Round Food	161
11	Putting it all Together	169

Introduction: Why Minimalism?

Since 2015 I have written books on composting, survival gardening, food forests and plant propagation, with the goal of taking complicated (and sometimes boring) topics and translating them into a form that can be immediately put to use by backyard gardeners. In the following book, we'll go even further by distilling gardening itself down to its very basics. This is a book of gardening philosophy designed to help you filter your agricultural ideas down to what you really need, keeping the wheat and blowing away the chaff.

Over the last year, the title of this book has changed from *Machete Gardening* to *Minimalist Gardening* to *Machete Gardening* and then back to *Minimalist Gardening*. I like the concept of a machete as being the most basic and universal of gardening tools. It's also used to clear away undergrowth and to cut pathways through the trackless wilderness, which ties into the minimalist idea of getting rid of unnecessary junk. Yet the title *Minimalist Gardening* is more trendy and directly states what this book is about, so it will probably sell better. (This is important, since our seed budget is insane.) So *Minimalist Gardening* it is.

Recently I took my wife to an estate sale in search of a nice bench for our front porch. There we wandered through the remains of a life.

Four outbuildings and two houses full of stuff. Hundreds of old prescriptions and nail polish bottles, piles of old keys, stacks of lumber and broken sports equipment. A half-dozen sewing machines. Dozens of pocketknives. Stacks of cheaply framed inspirational prints and quotes. Mass-market paperback devotionals and trashy romances. Boxes of Christmas decorations. A shed jammed with old 70's furniture. Rack after rack of inexpensive and dated clothing. The woman had died in her 80s, and her family didn't want all the piles of junk she had accumulated over decades of hoarding.

What profit did it all bring her? It was piles of stuff she had to navigate her way around for decades before her final exit. You can't take it with you. And even if you could, it would all look mighty tacky stacked up on the streets of gold.

Also, the bench I wanted sold before we got there, so I'm a little bitter about the whole thing.

Over the years, we've gotten less attached to "stuff," whether it be garden tools or collectibles, electronics or clothing. Hence, as I've gotten older, I'm embraced a more minimalist approach to everything. When you have a large family, it helps to have less stuff around, as there's less to clean and sort—and the children are more important than stuff.

I wouldn't call us extreme minimalists by any stretch. We still have a lot of stuff. But it's mostly things we use and like—and we regularly conduct purges to clean out everything unnecessary or unwanted from our lives. I suppose you could call us Minimalist catechumens who are striving to go deeper into the world of less.

When you think of Minimalism, you might picture a perfectly clean and almost empty apartment, decorated in white and gray, with a single sofa and a small table. On the table is a MacBook and a cup of coffee in a white mug, and the only other decor is a potted fiddleleaf fig in one corner. Or a monstera. If there's a fiddleleaf and a monstera, you're dealing with a minimalist hoarder.

There is a great draw towards living minimally, especially on a day where you've suffered a Lego-related foot injury while navigating through the downstairs hallway. It's also appealing when you look around and see all the items in your house that need to be washed, dusted, vacuumed, repaired, sorted, put away, oiled, reattached, painted, etc. Japanese minimalist Fumio Sasaki writes in *Goodbye, Things* that everything in your house is sending you silent messages:

> Things don't just sit there. They send us silent messages. And the more the item has been neglected, the stronger its message will be.
>
> Maybe there's an English textbook that I gave up on before I even got halfway through it. It might be looking at me now and saying something like *You look bored. Why don't you try to study me again?*
>
> Or there's a dead lightbulb that has yet to be replaced:

Don't tell me you forgot to buy my replacement yet again! *Why can't you do something so simple?*

Or a stack of dirty dishes: *Here we go again. I can never count on you.*

We even get messages from items we use on a daily basis. Imagine what your TV might be saying to you: *Uh, you have a bunch of recordings you haven't watched yet. Oh, and maybe it's about time you gave me a light dusting.*

And your laptop: *It sure would be nice to have a printer as a friend... oh well, nevermind.*

And there's the body soap in the bathroom: *Excuse me, I'm running out!*

As to the bedsheets: *I know you're busy, but would you mind giving me a wash one of these days soon?*

All of our possessions want to be cared for, and they tell us that every time we look at them. They begin to form lines in our head, waiting their turn for us to really look at them and listen to what they have to say.

This line of things gets longer and longer as we acquire more material possessions. I call that list the "silent to-do list."

Your stuff has a way of controlling you, and sending half or more of what you own to the thrift store (and/or the dump) feels freeing. We've done it multiple times, as stuff has a way of building up and keeping us from the clean house and the simple life we desire.

Minimalism makes you ask the question, "What do I need?" Further, it makes you think about what brings you joy. We

INTRODUCTION: WHY MINIMALISM?

find a lot of joy in our garden, but we have to seek to remove discordant notes from the space—junk!—or else it just becomes ugly and less satisfying.

So: does your garden space bring you joy?

The "Dean of Clean" Don Aslett writes in *Clutter's Last Stand*:

> We all hate junky yards–even someone whose yard looks like the city dump will, then viewing another sloppy, junk-plastered yard, squint his eyes and say, "What a disgrace, just look at all that trash! They must be real slobs."
>
> You feel the same way, don't you? But how is *your* yard? Is it an All-American avalanche of "antiques"?
>
> Right out the back door, junk starts with rusted or broken wind chimes, deceased weather instruments, bent-back awnings covered with sagging lattice, a slum birdhouse or two in condemned condition, a lean-to shed bulging with sun-cracked hoses, handleless tools, and rotting stakes and baskets. Against the fence are an abandoned rabbit cage, car parts, and decaying barrels. Then there is a coy cherub fountain, unhung hanging baskets, some broken aluminum lounge chairs, a mound of salvaged bricks and blocks, a peeling Paul Revere light post, and a couple of faded plastic squirrels. And oh, yes–that pile of boards scrounged out of a junk pile, worn not from age, but from ten years of being moved around to more inconspicuous places. Let's not overlook those twirling plastic sunflowers, tire tulip beds, miniature white plastic picket fences, rusted swing-sets, abandoned outgrown swimming pools, rusted grills from the past three seasons, and the TV antenna

that toppled during the worst storm of the 90's. Not to mention last year's Christmas tree; outdoor Christmas lights standing fast in July; and overgrown and untrimmed, dying, dead, shrubbery.

Your garden already needs regular care even when it's *not* a junky mess! It can pull at you and take your time, crying at you to be planted and weeded and hoed. Add onto that our tendency to pick up way more gardening tools and junk than we need, from duplicate rakes to broken tillers, to old pots in piles. More than that, we also spend time and effort creating elaborate systems that aren't necessary to our primary goal of growing food.

Let's cut all that junk out of our lives. Let's return our gardening to something beautiful and simple. Something that improves our lives and makes them better, rather than dragging us down. And it's not just about the junk—we also need to back up and ask ourselves if all the complicated systems we're being sold are necessary to meet the goal of food production.

Hint: they aren't.

Here's another benefit of minimalizing your garden junk and your approach to gardening. If the complexity of the system is minimal, there are less potential points at which your food production can break down, making it likely to sail through hard times—or even do better in them. That's another blessing.

INTRODUCTION: WHY MINIMALISM?   vii

While waiting for a flight out of Grenada during the midst of the 2020 pandemic, I read the book *Antifragile* by Nicolas Nassim Taleb. Much of his thinking on the tail risks of complicated systems and financial markets meshed with my own observations in my backyard gardens.

High-tech doesn't always mean "better." Often it makes things worse, though perhaps not at the beginning. Complicated, centralized systems with lots of moving parts contain many potential breakdown points that are often unseen until the wheels blow off.

"No one could have seen this coming!" is a common refrain after a market crash.

Do you recall the build up to the mortgage crisis in the late 2000s? I remember being told by someone in 2006 that his Florida townhome had doubled in the last couple of years. Since I was a bit of an economics junkie and knew we were in a boom, I advised him to sell it.

He laughed. "Are you kidding? It keeps going up! A thousand people a day are moving to Florida!"

Just a few short years later, the value of his townhome was less than what he'd paid for it. Worse, the townhome community was in crisis, as many owners were being foreclosed upon or had just walked away. Now larger and larger community assessments had to be made on the remaining owners to keep the utilities on.

It was a mess. In good times as a "rising tide lifts all boats," the complexity of shared ownership with multiple individuals could be managed. Everyone was getting richer together. But once the banks broke the financial system, the unexpected shock caused many to be thrown out of the boat, and the remaining sailors could hardly bail fast enough to save the vessel.

Of course, years later, that bubble has more than reinflated. And we're probably headed for another pop, which should motivate us to simplify now and grow our own food with tried-and-true methods.

The goal of this book is to help you make your gardens not only resilient but *antifragile*, as Taleb would put it—and we'll reach that goal by being minimal in what we do, removing what is unnecessary and making more happen with less. For years we have experimented with simple systems for cutting the fat out of gardening and reducing it to its basics. The goal is to have a garden that will not only survive but thrive in tough times when more complex systems are failing.

Our approach to gardening minimalism is a three-fold cord of simplicity, practicality and antifragility.

With that in mind, let's grab our machetes and start slashing away all the junk we don't need.

Chapter 1

Complexity, Engineers vs. Rastas, and Remembering the Point

We have owned multiple tillers over the years. At times, they have served us well. At many other times, they have caused me to say certain words that are generally recognized as being unfit for polite company.

We gave up on owning a tiller for almost a decade, and our main tilling implement was a Meadow Creature broadfork, with some extra assistance from a long-handled pointed hoe we bought from EasyDigging.com.

But broadforking new ground with thick sod takes quite a bit of time. So when I wanted to create a large garden area on our current homestead, I called my friend James, who then brought over his tractor and tilled it for us.

Ergo, David The Good's minimalist solution for installing a new garden is to *outsource it to someone with a Kubota*.

Yes, it's funny. Especially since I am an advocate of using hand tools and simple solutions. But sometimes the simplest solution is to recruit someone in your community with a big power tool. Smaller tillers are generally consumer-grade tools and are prone to breaking. Tractors are a different animal altogether. People have seen me borrowing a tractor in the past and complained that not everyone has access to a tractor. How dare I?

It's true that not everyone has a tractor or access to one. Or a tiller, for that matter. But that doesn't mean you shouldn't use one if you can. If I didn't have James to help me till with the tractor, I would have gone to the hardware store in town and rented a tiller for the day. If I didn't have a hardware store in town with a tiller available for rent, I would have broadforked the entire area over a period of time. Fortunately, we had James. And, a few months later, I caught a sale just before New Years' and got a brand-new rear tine tiller for half its retail price.

Some people don't have access to clean drinking water, but that doesn't mean you only have to drink bottled water in some sort of solidarity with those lacking safe tap water or a clean well. If you have the opportunity to get something done, go for it.

Still—I don't need to own a tractor. Or a tiller. The latter is really only useful when gardening on a large scale or breaking new ground, and the former, though very useful for a wide range of tasks, is currently too expensive for our budget.

I know this, because out of curiosity I looked into the price of buying a Kubota like the one James effortlessly used to tear through our sod. *Wouldn't it be fun to own a tractor?* I thought. I could dig trenches with it, and move rocks, and till, and bush-hog and knock over popcorn trees in the woods by the pond. That would be great!

I looked it up. At about $35,000, I would be able to do all those things. That would get me the tractor, the turf tires, the bucket on the front, the tiller attachment and the bushhog deck.

No. There's no way. I can't justify it. Unless, perhaps, this book sells 100,000 copies. Then I'll think about it.

Now if you find a screaming deal on a tractor, or if you're managing a large space, or if you use it for work—like James— and it will be worth it, go for it! There's nothing wrong with buying a tractor. Yet it is another thing you have to maintain and feed and care for.

Look, if I could get a tractor with everything I wanted for less than the value of the veggies it would help me grow in a couple of years, I would go for it. Just resist the urge to blow money and go for complexity right from the beginning. And remember: a tractor needs diesel to keep running, and it also needs parts which are manufactured far away. With how complicated and unstable the world has been lately, I would not trust a tractor as my only tool for the preparation of gardens, as it becomes an expensive yard ornament if fuel supplies fail. If you really want a tiller and will use it, go ahead and get one. But first I would start with the simple things: a spade, a fork, a broadfork and a grub hoe, and a machete.

Harder times can actually make for better—antifragile—gardens.

How so?

Because if you're living in easy times, you just borrow a tiller and buy some 10-10-10 or some organic amendments. This is the lazier way to get things done, but it's not the ideal way to get things done. A double-dug bed with compost is a better planting space than a tilled bed with 10-10-10. A broadfork's tines loosen soil deeper than a tractor's tiller. They also cause much less soil disturbance.

Homemade compost is simpler but takes more work than buying nutrients in bags—yet it's better. During the pandemic, we dug beds with a broadfork and made compost from bamboo leaves and sawdust mixed with the contents of our composting toilet system. It was a very antifragile garden, but under lockdowns, that was all we could make. We also mulched with leaves raked from the jungle. The garden grew marvelously, as we were pushed by the system to work harder and to be minimalist. Hand tools and homemade compost are powerful things. That simplicity is hard to break. Even if an EMP took out the power grid and we had no money left in the bank, we'd still have food.

Know the Simple Before Pursuing the Complex

Gardening seems basic at the beginning. You start with seeds, soil, sunshine and water. Plant a seed and water it and it comes up. It grows, then eventually you harvest it when it's made whatever you want, whether that's a root, a fruit, salad greens or string beans.

Yet gardening rapidly spirals into fractals of complexity as you learn more. What seeds will you plant? Which variety? Are the seed hybrids or open pollinated? What time of year? How rich does the soil need to be? Does the plant prefer sun, half-shade or shade? Does it need lots of water or does it rot with lots of water? Is it an annual or a perennial? How do you know when a melon is ready? When do you harvest English peas? How close do you space your seeds? Is it frost-tender or hardy? Can it take the heat? What about companion planting? What about mold? What about moles? What about voles? Do they need to grow on poles? Why are the leaves full of holes?

Every crop has different needs, and they bear on different schedules.

The difference between two crops can be huge. Like bananas and oranges, for example. Bananas love lots of water and lots of soil fertility. I've seen clumps of them growing in water overflowing from a spring. Each banana trunk is actually a pseudo-stem, more like a lily than a tree, growing from a big central root that is capable of making many shoots just like it. When a banana "tree" fruits, it's done. You cut the entire banana trunk down to the ground when you harvest and then the plant grows more trunks. They love hot weather and basically quit growing when the temperatures drop into the 60s. At 32 degrees, they start showing damage and will often lose their fruit. They don't have a specific time of fruiting but will fruit when they are big enough and jolly well feel like it. Bananas can't be successfully grafted.

Simon Maughan of the Royal Horticultural Society writes:

> For a graft to unite, the root stock and the piece of shoot to be attached to it must both possess cambial tissue, a thin layer of cells inside the vascular bundles that divide to create a successful union. Monocotyledonous plants (bananas, palm trees, lilies, grasses and so on) do not possess a cambium, however, and grafts are therefore very difficult to achieve. If successful, the two cut surfaces must be held permanently together by tying or taping, which in all likelihood would further increase the chance of disease.[1]

Now compare the banana with an orange tree. An orange can grow in the same climate as a banana, but will also survive further north. If you overwater orange trees, they will yellow and may die. They also don't need near as much nitrogen to do well. Orange trees are a *real* tree, with a woody trunk and leaves. If you cut one to the ground, it will take a long time to grow back and certainly won't regrow and fruit the same year, like bananas will. Oranges have a specific season in which they fruit and that's it. They are often grafted, many times onto their scrappy relative the trifoliate orange.

If you try to grow oranges like bananas or bananas like oranges, they won't be happy. Over the course of my gardening career, if I may assign such a label to my wanderings and backyard experiments, I have grown gardens in the tropics, in zone 11, in zone 9/10, in zone 8/9, in a solid zone 8 and in zone 6/7. That is—in order—Grenada, West Indies; Ft. Lauderdale, Florida; Frostproof, Florida; Anthony, Florida; Lower Alabama and in Smyrna, Tennessee. Each location had different benefits and challenges, with different soils, rainfall, frost dates (or no frosts at all!), and different species.

In Tennessee, we used deep mulching to loosen rocky clay soil and gardened Ruth Stout style. I planted fruit trees I never could have grown in sunny South Florida where I grew up, such as peaches, plums, apples and pears. We harvested Nanking cherries and champagne grapes from the backyard, along with abundant harvests of pears, tomatoes, Jerusalem artichokes and herbs. In our front yard we planted banks of tulips and daffodils which painted an Impressionist explosion of color in late winter and early spring. Though the soil was rocky clay, it was also rich, and the rains of spring turned all of nature into a verdant carpet of green. Summer was quite hot and usually dry. Winter, on the other hand, was a long, gray, rainy mess of red mud and lack of sunlight.

In Frostproof, we found the sand to be very poor and had the best luck growing cassava in the ground, along with various vegetables in containers. Over time we could have fought the sand and made some fantastic gardens, but we lived there for less than a year and didn't get a chance. Trees did better than annuals by a long shot. There we had also had the worst fire ant nests we've ever encountered. Any compost pile became a solid mass of stinging ants within a day, and ants would stream through the electrical outlets in our trailer to devour any crumbs left on the counter for more than a few minutes. On the other hand, bananas and guavas grew readily, along with Indian curry tree and true yams. Hot peppers loved the heat and sweet potatoes happily took over any space where they were planted. We lived in a small neighborhood surrounded by old orange groves, and the aroma of orange blossoms hung in the air deliciously, wafting past in the warm breezes. Wild edibles, from passionfruit species to Florida bully fruit were common. Bald eagles and alligators, armadillos and snakes were all part of the ecosystem.

In Grenada, we grew many tropical fruits which most gardeners only dream of growing, from vanilla orchids to soursop, breadfruit to coffee, cocoa to giant plantains. There we found that deep mulching would attract too many sprout-eating critters and kept us from direct-seeding plants. We also learned to garden on slopes, creating drains and shaping beds to shrug off hard rains. Perennials were king, with lots of taro, bananas, plantains, mangoes, starfruit, cassava, Mexican tree spinach and other long-lived plants in our gardens. The climate alternated between a dry, hot season, and a slightly cooler rainy season where anything would grow. Cutworms were a huge problem in the annual gardens, but trees were amazingly productive and low-care.

In South Florida, where my wife and I grew up and later lived for a time after our years in Tennessee, we found that we could grow our "normal" vegetables—like lettuce and green beans—in the winter, but in the summer they were destroyed by the heat and humidity. Yet in the summer, fruit trees and tropical plants thrive and grow so fast you could almost hear them growing. Kale in winter... cassava in summer! What a place! Most gardening books just don't apply in South Florida's unique climate, and if you follow the instructions on seed packets, you rarely have luck. Everything is different and the plants and planting times really have to fit the climate or you won't have luck. In Idaho, you could live on potatoes. In South Florida, you'd do better living on coconuts. Winter gardening was really the best for annuals, with the proper season for tomatoes, as an example, being from about November to March.

Where we currently live in Lower Alabama, we can also grow some crops through the winter but we also face excessive frost damage to even hardy plants, as the weather swings from the 80s down into the 20s in the same week. At our last home we dealt with nutrient-poor acid grid unworthy to be called soil. At our current—and hopefully last—house we have a dark gray sandy loam soil that grows thick grass and excellently supports most garden crops and fruit trees. We've hauled in buckets of cucumbers and potatoes and our fruit trees are growing quickly. Right now I have hundreds of sugarcane plants rapidly reaching for the sky as the rains of summer encourage them to maximum growth. Yet just a few miles away, we had great difficulty growing many of these crops due to the poor soil, which goes to show that not only is every climate different, every *backyard* is different! As a Minnesota gardener, you may have more in common with a Wisconsin gardener, but you probably don't have *everything* in common.

So what basic principles can we use across the board? Is there anything that just works?

Trying to simplify gardening back down to basic principles seems almost impossible, yet there are rules of (green) thumb you can use to cut out wasted time and effort and to bring some much-needed simplicity back into your food growing.

Plant Abundantly and Let God Sort it Out

If you only have one apple tree, you're likely to worry about it. If fireblight strikes or a storm blows it down, you're out of apples. And if you planted it ten years ago, that's a lot of time down the drain.

So don't plant just one. Plant many. Plant more than you could ever use. Cover your yard with figs and pears and grapes and blackberries, walnuts and blueberries, lemons, plums, cherries. Don't fiddle around and think small. Go crazy.

I recently visited my friend Randall's homestead (he and his wife are "Flomaton Famous" on YouTube) and saw his large collection of plants. In the shade of larger trees and around his patio were hot peppers and edible cacti, loquat trees, gingers, turmerics, figs, citrus and many more useful and edible species.

He asked if I wanted a few plants and I said sure. We ended up going home with about thirty different trees and plants without making a dent in his collection. Out in the yard he has rows of figs and large clumps of bananas, apples, plums, pears, pecans, tea, grapefruit, kumquats and much more. It's abundant, and there is plenty to eat and to share.

You might think this could get expensive. Yes, it could, *if you are buying lots of plants from nurseries.* In that case, you are trading money for time. It took them time to grow out those plants, so you pay them for their work and their babysitting and marketing of the potted plants you drive back home in the trunk of your car.

If you instead bought a load of potting soil and bulk pots, you could literally propagate a thousand dollars worth of plants in a weekend. Learn to grow trees from seed. Learn to graft. Learn to air-layer. Learn to start cuttings. Next thing you know, you've got plenty of trees to plant our in your yard and to experiment with. If a tree costs you almost nothing, there's no pain in using it for an experiment. What about planting a hedge of loquats? Or running grapevines up into a walnut tree? Or planting three apple trees in one hole? Or buying the empty lot next door and covering the entire thing with a food forest? You can do it without being too precious about individual plants.

The same goes for your vegetable gardens. Buy more seeds than you need, plant plenty, then thin, leaving only the best in the garden. Transplants are expensive, but seeds are cheap. If there's a plant you really like and it's expensive, buy one, then propagate lots more. You can plant, give away or sell the ones you don't need, paying yourself back for the original purchase.

Have you ever noticed the density of a forest's edge? Think about growing that way. Plant lots of things and see what survives. If you're paying $40 per fruit tree, that's insane. But if you paying pennies for soil and pots and growing your own, you can afford to be luxuriant in your planting. You can throw species at your yard that are marginal for your region and see if they work. If you're buying a chestnut tree in a pot, it's expensive. But if you plant 40 chestnuts from seed, you can put them here, there and everywhere. I currently have a couple dozen pawpaw trees I started from seed that are waiting to be planted out in the yard. That's way cheaper than buying larger ones in pots. I really know very little about growing pawpaws, but I have *24 chances to get it right*.

Overplant and quit worrying about individual plants so much. You can always make more.

Don't Use a Complicated System When a Simpler One Will Suffice

The other day I saw a ridiculous garden design in a social media post. It was made from perhaps a dozen five-gallon buckets with holes drilled in them, arranged in three tiers. They were all screwed into a wooden frame of 2x4s with 4x4 legs at the corners. I added up the cost in my head. 12 buckets, at $5 per bucket, with maybe $120 in wood. So... $180 in wood and plastic. And that's before you add six bags of potting soil.

Still, it's neat, right?

But come on. That's really only about twelve square feet of growing space. Think about it! Even Mel Bartholomew's simple 4' x 4' Square Foot Garden has more space than that and costs less to create.

There is a certain personality—I call it the "engineer" personality—that can't stand doing things the simple way.

The simplest way to garden is to dig in the soil and plant seeds. The engineer personality says, "No, that's not good enough! I must come up with something more complicated and scientific! Something that overcomes the problem of weeds and gives the plants perfect soil. Something that can grow salads on my back patio next to my treadmill-driven compost tumbler and my solar dehydrator (which for some reason keeps causing blueberries to mold—venting issue, perhaps—must continue researching and do a rebuild!) and my lawnmower solar charging station!"

Yet, I must say, I am not picking on all engineers. I love engineers. I am particularly fond of running water, the internal combustion engine and the LibreOffice software I use to write my books.

Yet some engineers have an undeniable penchant for adding unneeded complexity to systems. Why would you make a three-tiered bucket garden thing when you could just grow in the ground? Or buy a simple horse trough for about the same price, which you could fill with perfect dirt and garden in for the next thirty years?

Engineer-minded gardeners send me emails showing robots doing weeding and irrigation systems with artificial leaves that serve as a proxy sensor for the leaves of actual plants, ensuring the perfect amount of moisture reaches your hydrangea collection.

It's fascinating. Yet in this man-made complexity there is a huge potential for breakdown. The proliferation of moving parts exponentially increases the avenues for failure. It is less antifragile than using systems which have existed for millennia.

As my friend Rick Morris notes: "Any engineering solution that has been commonly used for decades after the novelty wore off, is generally a good one. That's the test."

Sometimes a piece of technology actually makes a job easier, but is not as antifragile.

Agrarian philosopher Wendell Berry prefers draft horses to tractors. They are also fueled by grass rather than diesel, which requires no drilling, refining, shipping or money to obtain. Horses also don't need parts from China, and can make new horses. Tractors, obviously, cannot.

As my friend Jack once related:

> Back in college, in an Engineering class, the prof was giving his lecture when he was interrupted by the sound of a leaf

blower. The landscaping crew was at work, and the open door (it was hot) meant the noise was pretty loud in the lecture hall. He stopped, walked over, closed the door, then resumed. "It occurs to me that we aren't teaching a fundament element of engineering. If there's already a solution to a problem, don't create something worse. A broom works fine."

Yet, it must be stated, that the easiest way to do something is not always the most antifragile.

A broom or a draft horse may be antifragile, in that they can be locally produced, are simple enough to continue using even if supply lines break, don't require fuel from external sources, will be used more during a crisis, etc. But they aren't easy. A man can get a ton of work done on a tractor in a short period of time. So long as there's fuel and parts to keep it running, it takes much less of his life to get a lot more done. The same goes for a leaf blower. If you've ever swept a long driveway after mowing the lawn—and compared how long that takes to using a leaf-blower—you know what I mean.

One can argue that there are secondary benefits to sweeping, such as not spending money on a leaf-blower, saving the user's hearing, and proving the sweeper with some physical exercise; however, running the leaf-blower means he can get a large area done quickly and efficiently and then go in and drink some iced tea.

There is a balance between the easiest way to do something and the most antifragile way, as well as the most minimalist way. They do not always line up, so we must pick and choose how we're going to spend our days.

The most prudent of choices is to learn the simple tools first and to keep them as backups for the less simple.

If you feel the need to own and use a tiller, also be sure to have a spade and fork as a backup option. You should also know how to create a no-till garden. In the event of your tiller breaking or the supply lines making parts impossible to find, you can still grow food.

Some of the super easy things have strings attached. There are lots of strings attached to reading a book on your smartphone. Your battery must be working, you have to trust that it's not being surreptitiously edited if it's owned by an entity such as Amazon, you have to keep up with your monthly phone plan, you must own a phone, etc. The phone is a very easy way to store a ton of books, but there are many strings attached to it.

A paperback book in your possession has no strings attached. You can pick it up and read it and it won't be deleted or changed, it does not need servicing or a monthly payment plan, it does not emit a glow that is damaging to your eyes, etc.

But it's bulky and not as convenient. Particularly when you consider that an entire gigantic library can be stored on the average smartphone.

It's all about balance. It's also about preferences.

Sometimes I am asked questions such as "why do you bend down to plant seeds instead of saving your back?" and "why are you digging by hand instead of using that tractor you were borrowing?" and "why don't you carry all that in a wheelbarrow?"

The answer is that by doing manual labor I am able to skip going to the gym and to keep my body functioning better for longer.

An obese man once told me I was working too hard and that I needed to get a tractor like his instead. I told him that part of the reason I worked with hand tools was to stay fit. He jokingly told me, "Oh no... you should just use a tractor so you can be fat like me!"

It's funny, but it's not funny. Sometimes the minimalist approach also allows you to consolidate two activities together, such as gardening and physical fitness. It feels good to work hard and to sweat. To feel your muscles work. To realize you "still got it," and will continue to have it so long as you don't give in to ease and convenience.

When I visited in East Timor in 2019, an American missionary pointed out an Indonesian woman and her daughter walking alongside the road hauling water from a well to their home.

"It's so sad that they have to work so hard," she said. "That little girl is helping her mom carry water for over a mile."

It was hot and dusty and it was certainly hard work. But something struck me as I watched them.

If that girl had been in the states, she would probably have an unhealthy diet and weight, and be separated from her mom in either daycare or school or both. Instead, she was strong and was spending quality time with her mom, accomplishing an act of service for her family.

Which is better? Obese children with lives of ease, glued to smartphones and separated from their families? Or hard-working children with their parents, serving their families in the absence of TikTok and Instagram?

Yes, it's hard work. But hard work can be good for the soul. This may be too simplistic, as there are also problems with malnourishment in Indonesia, yet there are multiple ways to look at each situation. Sometimes saving yourself or others from work is not the correct solution.

Though I would still prefer to have a leaf-blower so I don't have to spend an hour sweeping the carport, the porch and the driveway.

You know what? I'm gonna stop right here and go buy a leaf-blower. I've talked myself into it.

.

.

.

.

.

Okay, I'm back. I got one that used the same battery platform as our drill and driver set. Now I'm going to go waste 13.2 hours watching TikTok and eating Cheezits.

But back to the point! When you have an easy-to-use piece of technology, *it may be minimalist to use it*. Just remember the strings that are attached, and that sometimes the harder approach is more antifragile and/or may have additional side benefits.

Fumio Sasaki shares how he minimalized his life by getting rid of almost everything he owned.

He notes:

> The invention of the smartphone means we can carry around a cell phone, camera, TV, audio device, game console, watch, calendar, flashlight, map, or even noteppad, all in one little rectangle. It's also a compass, train timetable, dictionary, thick mail-order catalog, checkbook, or airline ticket. The first iPhone was introduced in Japan in 2007. I think the invention of the smartphone paved the way for all the minimalists we see around us today. No matter how vigorously a minimalist may throw away their possessions, their smartphone is often one of the last items to go (if it goes at all), because it obviously serves so many purposes.

It's true—it's a major part of our lives and has simplified a lot. However, I got rid of my smart phone two years ago and it made my life better.

At the beginning of 2022, I pulled the SIM card from my Android smartphone and said goodbye. That SIM card was then inserted into a Light Phone II. All that phone really does is text and call, though it also has a simple map app which provides simple written directions from location to location.

This was a very good decision for me and I do not regret it. Our phones are spy devices that track us and record our lives. They also constantly irradiate us. And yes, the Light Phone II also allows the user to be tracked, but most of the time I leave it off or at home. It's actually kind of a pain to use the darn thing, but I am grateful for it.

Once you're not checking notifications and emails and reading the news, etc., you stop caring about your phone.

Don't you remember what it was like to not carry your life around in your pocket? To not constantly have your eyes and attention drawn to a little screen that begs for your attention? To live life unencumbered by digital noise?

I remembered, and wished I had those days back. So I reclaimed them by ditching my phone.

The benefits of living without a digital chain greatly outweigh the difficulties. I've gotten to read many more books since I cut the leash. (You can see my reading list on the margin of my blog at thesurvivalgardener.com.)

My wife still has a smart phone which she uses. We take photos with it, and occasionally I'll take it in the car when driving someplace unfamiliar.

But personally, I'm done. And if her phone was gone too, it'd be fine.

I can sit by the pond and watch my cows without Zuckerberg dinging away in my pocket. I play with my children without taking a phone from my pocket. I go to sleep without the blue glow of a screen.

Is it minimal? Maybe not. Does it make life better? In my case, yes. Your mileage may vary. It took me years to become independent enough that I could afford to ditch the phone.

And should we really rely on a piece of technology to outsource so much of our lives? That's a question we all need to answer. A phone makes many things easier when well-used (GPS, anyone?), and also brings in a stream of filth and covetousness and addiction and bad news, etc., if misused.

Sometimes—perhaps even often!—it's better for the soul to do things the hard way. We can't use convenience as our primary metric.

And some of these modern technologies may eventually be gone, replaced with something else. This age of high-tech might just be a blip before a new era of decentralized agrarianism takes over, or an EMP strike, or a massive plague, or who knows what?

It's safer to remain philosophically minimalist and know how to do things without high technology and without strings—though we can still enjoy the technology while we have it. There is not necessarily good or bad in the tech. You'll need to determine your goals and needs and preferences for yourself. But it is important to remember that many pieces of old technology will continue to be used far into the future, perhaps even when the shiny new things have failed or passed like hula-hooping, Beanie Babies and Pogs.

As Nicolas Nassim Taleb shares in *Antifragile*, the Lindy Effect posits that:

A technology, or anything nonperishable, increases in life expectancy with every day of its life–unlike perishable items (such as humans, cats, dogs, and tomatoes). So a book that has been a hundred years in print is likely to stay in print another hundred years.

Taleb illustrates this in one case by sharing how:

(Physicist Richard Gott) made a list of Broadway shows on a given day, May 17th, 1993, and predicted that the longest-running ones would last longest, and vice-versa. He was proven right with 95 percent accuracy. He had, as a child, visited both the Great Pyramid (fifty-seven hundred years old), and the Berlin Wall (twelve years old), and correctly guessed that the former would outlive the latter.

Rastas vs. Professors

With this in mind, let's beat a dead horse and consider the case of aquaponics vs. traditional gardening.

When I first discovered aquaponics, I was fascinated. The idea of raising fish and vegetables in a closed loop was eye-opening. This could be the food revolution of the future!

In an aquaponics system, a gardener raises fish in tanks. The water of the tanks is pumped through beds of plants and sent back to the fish with much of the nitrates removed and used for plant growth, cleaning the water and keeping the fish (usually tilapia) happy.

In a nutshell, the fish create waste and the plants use that waste to grow—and you get a crop of meat and vegetables from your aquaponics garden.

The system sounds easy and fun. The plants never wilt and never need feeding, thanks to the always flowing water around their roots. The fish grow and provide you with all the meat you'll ever need in a much smaller space than a traditional pond.

Yet over the years, I have gone from cautiously enthusiastic to downright opposed to aquaponics as I've seen multiple systems created by multiple people and organizations, and seen very little to recommend them as a viable alternative to growing in the ground.

One friend has had all his fish killed multiple times due to failed pumps and drains. Another friend has worked with aquaponics in his backyard as a hobby for years for very little return in fish.

When we were in the Caribbean, there was a non-profit organization promoting aquaponics systems and installing them at schools as part of a "food security" outreach. They even had grant money for it. They legitimately thought it was a great idea and a revolution and all that nonsense. The frustrating thing is that they were promoting this mess of complicated plastic and pumps in a place where the soil is rich, the climate is mild, and there are millions of fish in the sea.

The demonstration garden a professor built on the island featured a few anemic salad greens and tomatoes and a few fish that had managed to survive in the tank. They had to be fed by a paid employee at the facility where the garden was housed. Yet nearby there were huge stands of bananas, mangoes and breadfruit. Illiterate Rastafarian farmers would smoke ganja in the morning, then go up on the hillside and use a grub hoe to make a few mounded garden beds and plant yams in them. Through the year, they'd put in a few stakes and keep the weeds down with a machete, then during the Christmas season they'd dig up hundreds of pounds of calorie-rich roots. They could harvest 100,000 calories in the same space an aquaponics system would take up, without imported PVC piping, a solar panel and pump, gravel and plastic tanks, and fish that would kick off when someone sneezed.

Dirt. A grub hoe. A machete. Some sticks. Pieces of yams. With an optional shot of Clarke's white rum and a ganja cigarette. And you get food security. And we're not even talking about the variety of things that can be grown in the ground compared to in an aquaponics setup. Deep-rooted high-calorie crops were not possible in those gravel beds. Instead you had lettuce and basil and tomatoes. Those won't fill you up.

It makes more sense to plant a bed of yams and go fishing in a river rather than attempting to balance pH and water levels and breed fish in a tank.

And yet a farmer could get even more simple. Don't worry about yams and beds and hoeing. Just plant coconuts, plantains and breadfruit. One breadfruit tree cost a couple of American dollars at the local government nursery and would produce hundreds of pounds of high-quality food a year with no work once established. And it would do that *for a generation or more*. Add a pig beneath a mango tree to eat the fallen fruits and you get pork as well.

No pipes. No fish. No over-engineered plastic mess.

When gauged by the Lindy Effect, which system is likely to last longer: PVC-constructed aquaponics with its pumps, imported fish and regular water testing, or traditional gardening in the soil?

How simple can we make things?

How profitable?

According to a report on the Economics of Aquaponics by the Southern Regional Aquaculture Center:

> The most challenging aspect of managing an aquaponics operation is to develop a realistic, accurate, and workable marketing plan. Raising fish indoors is two to three times more expensive than raising fish in open ponds. Thus, a profitable aquaponics operation will need to seek out and develop a market that will pay a higher- than-average price for the crop. An in-depth understanding of the level and type of competition in the market place is essential. For example, an individual who raises lettuce in aquaponics will need to compete with lettuce sold in WalMart, in other grocery stores, and at farmers' markets. Why would an individual buy aquaponically grown lettuce, especially if it is more expensive than other types? The seller must have a clear answer to that question to be competitive.

> A second marketing consideration is that the type of high-end market that will pay a premium price will also entail greater marketing costs. For example, if the freshness of the produce is a main reason for a top chef to pay a premium price for aquaponically raised herbs, that chef may want frequent deliveries to ensure that freshness. Frequent deliveries will require additional personnel, vehicles, and associated mileage expenses.
>
> Labor requirements must also be considered. An aquaponics system requires frequent attention. Even on a small scale, aquaponics systems are complex because of their multiple components and requirements. Disease prevention, water level control, and preventing rodents and other problems require inspection and care of the system throughout the day, 7 days a week.

Yet even if you manage to work out these details, the report further notes:

> ...the fish portion of the aquaponics system was not profitable, with the production costs of tilapia less than market price in only one study, and either higher or essentially the same in the others. This also is consistent with anecdotal reports that the fish portion of aquaponic systems tends to be a net loss, with profits primarily from the vegetable portion.[2]

And the profit margins from the vegetable portion aren't all that hot.

When I was working on a college newspaper long ago, the journalism professor overseeing the paper hung a sign on the wall that read "K.I.S.S.: Keep It Simple Stupid!" He could have been a Rasta! The idea is to avoid cluttering up your stories with needless detail. If a murder witness shares his story, you don't have to note that the witness wore "Nike tennis shoes, stonewashed boot cut jeans and a navy blue dress shirt with a repeating *Monstera* leaf pattern," (unless perhaps you're covering a murder at a fashion show).

When you add lots of pipes and aeration and electricity and fish and gravel and valves, etc., etc., etc., to your garden, you make the system complicated. This isn't to say it won't work, but it does allow in many more chances for error and problems.

The argument that amazes me is: "Aquaponics makes sense!" No, it doesn't, except in certain applications. It's a needless cluttering of gardening. It appeals to smart people who like to tinker, but that doesn't make it better than forking up a bed and planting seeds in the ground. Or going no-till and just adding compost on top of in-ground slightly mounded beds, like Charles Dowding.

Some of us really like to build things and create systems and that's fine. You are not necessarily a bad person because you like aquaponics. It's an indicator of a serious personality disorder, but it doesn't mean you're evil and/or stupid. It may be a fun hobby—like building model train sets—but from my observations over the years, it's an inferior form of

gardening that presents itself as superior due to its flashiness and scientific veneer. Once you shell out the time and labor and money for parts, you are in the hole. When your fish die because the pump seized up, you are further in the hole. And also—I've seen a lot of sad, yellowing plants in aquaponics systems. Tweaking that fish/vegetable loop isn't easy, even though it seems perfect in theory.

Returning to our Rasta friend, you could give him a shovel, a hoe, some seeds, sunshine and water and he'll grow plenty of food without spending much time or money. He can plant corn or yams and walk away for a week or two, then come back and spend a little time weeding, then walk away again.

You can't do that with aquaponics. And promoting it in the third world as a great alternative agricultural method is beyond silly. Tons of plastic and Styrofoam and more plastic, and more dependence on international manufacturing rather than local production. The local Rasta has skin in the game. If his garden doesn't grow, he will be hungry and will not have produce to sell at market. The overseas aquaponics promoters don't go hungry if their system fails in the hands of the people they give it to.

Farmers know how to grow food already, without first world nations spending money and promotional time to explain why they should switch to touchy and complicated systems based on plastic and technology. It's hubris: we know better than you—and we know better than nature! And look at how impressive all this is to newbies! It is SCIENCE!

You could create a simple in-ground garden for a few dollars, a few afternoons hard work and zero plastic. It's not science. It's scientism. It appears sciencey, and that is the lure.

It's like those weird products you see on late-night infomercials. "Never peel an egg by hand again!" My wife's brother gave her one of those egg-peelers. You're supposed to put a hard-boiled egg in it and hit the plunger, then the egg comes out nicely shelled.

We tried it and discovered it was excellent at transforming an egg into an instant egg salad complete with high-calcium shrapnel.

Another thing happens when we turn to aquaponics or hydroponics, or try to mix a "perfect" soil mix or use a soilless medium: we lose the soil ecosystem. Beneath the roots of our plants is a startlingly complex web of life. Fungi, bacteria and a huge amount of microlife lurk around the roots of our soil-planted crops.

We know very little about how this ecosystem works, but we do know that certain fungi connect with the roots of certain plants, trading minerals for sugars. We also know that some bacteria create colonies on the roots of some plants and trade nitrogen for sugars. The interaction between plants and soil life also stimulates plants to create certain compounds that may not be created in a more sterile system.

Will a tomato be as nutritionally dense if grown in a solution where you completely control the fertilization? Some tests show high sugar and flavor is achievable in a soilless system, but is it really as good for you? What about the various compounds created by a tomato living in a vast community of organisms?

I don't know. But I prefer the simple—and to play God less—as we don't even begin to comprehend all the moving pieces in the soil. Who knows what we may be missing?

Stay on Target

For most of us backyard vegetable gardeners, the point of our gardens is to grow food. We also embrace a secondary point in food-growing: we want food for our family that is not contaminated with herbicides and pesticides. We would also like that food to be as nutrient-dense as possible.

Additionally, we view our gardens as our in-ground survival food supply. It's a big savings account of calories which works as an insurance policy against hard times, should they come. If they don't, at least we're eating excellent food and saving money.

But why are you gardening? What is the driving desire behind your desire to grow food? What is the *point*?

For some people, gardening is just a relaxing outdoor activity that has the side benefit of producing some tasty tomatoes or strawberries, or a bit of oregano and basil for a home-made pizza. For others, the garden an integral part of a preparedness program—a bulwark against societal collapse, like owning a good AR-15 (with a red dot and tac light along with 20+ mags and a modest 25,000 rounds of ammo), a Geiger counter, and a solid early 80s M1 Abrams tank with low mileage.

Sometimes the garden is a place to grow a specific thing that brings glory to its owner, such as a giant pumpkin or the best homegrown salsa in town. Other times the garden is a backyard homeschool lesson where children can learn about how food grows.

One gardener might use Sevin dust and Malathion to control pests, whereas his neighbor down the street might eschew all chemicals in his gardens. Another gardener loves his tiller, whereas yet another believes that digging in the garden is tantamount to genocide.

What is the point of your garden? If you can keep it in mind, you'll find satisfaction. Sometimes we lose sight of why we are doing things and they become a complicated chore rather than a thing of joy.

Generally, the main point of backyard gardening is growing food. When ideology or complexity interfere with that, perhaps it's time to re-assess. I regularly encounter people that seem to spend all their time online getting in fights about their favorite methods and gardening personalities, yet they aren't really out there *doing* anything. Go do something, then talk.

One commenter watched one of my videos on growing pumpkins and wrote, "I think if I had this situation like pumpkins and other things growing, I would cook them as a soup and prepare meals from homeless, to be donated. Just my opinion to share the natural bounty with the marginalized/unfortunate ones of the country."

To which my reply was, "Grow some food, then, and do it."

It's all well and good to make castles in the sky, imagining all you would do *if you actually did anything*, but it's better to *actually do something*.

When we were transplanted back to the US in the middle of 2020, we rented a house in Lower Alabama. Back in Grenada, my family and I built some beautiful Grocery Row Gardens and a food forest. We were using chop-and-drop and bamboo leaves for mulch and we had collected a wide variety of bananas and plantains. I was breeding pumpkins and testing tomato varieties—and we even had a composting toilet system and over 1,000 gallons of rainwater harvesting in the small cabins we'd built.

Then we left it for a place with crummy soil and a very different climate. The first thing I wanted to do after moving in was to get food growing. We were offered a tractor and tiller so we set to work. Instead of using a broadfork and compost, we tore up the ground and planted a lot of single rows of crops to secure our food supply. We limed the ground and threw down some 10-10-10, along with some micronutrients, and we were back in the food-growing business.

Since I have a YouTube channel, my gardening is always under scrutiny. I was informed that I shouldn't use chemical fertilizers, that using a tractor was cheating, that tilling the ground destroyed soil life, that I should watch Elaine Ingham lectures, that I should deep mulch, that I should be composting more... etc. etc. etc.

It didn't bother me. We were growing food, and there is a sliding scale of priorities that should be considered. The main point of gardening was to grow food for the family, especially in uncertain times. Using a tractor and putting in single rows and feeding them quickly so we reaped a harvest fulfilled that goal. The pandemic was still a real concern and supply lines were looking shaky. So we did our best at that time, getting the food growing first before worrying about getting the food-growing system perfect.

Over the next two years at the property, however, our gardening rapidly changed to fall more in line with our ideal practices. Compost piles were built, cover crops were planted, biochar was made, soil was tested, balanced micronutrients were added, swamp water barrels were made, a diverse range of species were interplanted and we replaced the 10-10-10 with much better alternatives.

Even if you start with a less than ideal garden, *at least you are growing food!* Don't forget that main goal. Don't get so hung up on the ideal that you miss the point completely.

Nothing is perfect anyhow. If something doesn't work, change it and work with it. This is one reason we create simple mounded garden beds. Mounded beds are easy to move and change. If we want to switch to single rows, or intensive 5'-wide beds, or plant a tree in the middle of the garden and plant a circle of ginger plants around it, it's no big deal. If we avoid complicated initial designs that require lots of construction, such as building raised beds out of cedar or stone, we have not made an expensive commitment to a system that may not be ideal for the way we use our gardens.

Analysis Paralysis

Also, if you are prone to extensive planning, there is a very real risk of analysis paralysis.

I remember the first time I called my now-wife Rachel, hoping to take her out on a date. I spent more time worrying about the call than actually making it. Sometimes all the planning is an excuse to avoid doing something that scares you.

"Let me plan this out first..."

No. Jump. Fortune favors the bold.

To begin a food forest, you could start by clearing or sheet-mulching an area to kill the grass, then putting in a cover crop, perhaps with a bunch of nitrogen-fixing tree seeds in it. Then start planting larger shrubs and trees in that area, letting paths form as you go. Again: if you're not buying everything from nurseries, this isn't hard. As the system grows, chop and drop and thin as you like and let the forest emerge iteratively.

This helps break gridlock, too. Many food forests never really get growing because of analysis paralysis. Start planting and sort it all out as you grow. It's better than putting in one or two trees a year and agonizing over where things grow.

Many times you'll see elaborate food forest designs that require lots of sketching and measuring and planning and then more planning, and then...

...well, you know, we ain't got time for all that.

If you want to start a super-easy garden, just go till up an area and make single rows 3' apart, planting whatever crops are at the right season to plant. Hoe down the weeds as they appear.

So long as you get food growing, you're way ahead of the pack. If you feel like you need to do a lot of planning, then go ahead and do it. There may be some benefits to that approach, like not accidentally planting a pecan next to a power pole, or in getting some really pretty garden beds out in front of your house that line up with your gazebo and driveway, but don't plan so much that you don't *do*.

However you like to grow, grow.

Some of you will thrive with perfect rows of beans, measured out to the inch; others enjoy mixing beans into their tomato beds, their landscaping and their flowerpots and seeing how they grow. Others prefer big, crazy food forest systems, while still others just want a pretty raised bed with some salad greens.

Just remember the point is growing food, and you can work towards the ideal of organic, nutrient-dense food as you go. I'm not endorsing repeated tillage and chemical fertilizers as a mainstay of your gardening. We don't do either most of the time. But when we needed food fast in case of emergency, we did what we could with what we had. Keep your goals in mind and don't sweat the small stuff.

Chapter 2

The Wide World of Raised Bed Gardening

Raised beds are quite common in little backyard gardens. They're easily the predominant method used by homeowners, and there are multiple reasons for that. Let's take a diversion into the realm of raised bed gardening with a great big sack of ideas we've gathered over the years. Though not all these ideas are truly minimalist, they may be useful to you, especially if you are gardening on rented land or in a small space.

Some of these may veer into container gardening, but we'll pretend that all of them are raised beds.

5-Gallon Bucket Gardens

Rachel and I lived in two different homes in Tennessee, both of them in the execrable town of Smyrna, where the soil was decent but the town was run by snakes.

While there, we experienced the joy of rocky red clay. A woman that worked in the local Lowes gardening center told me that she had great luck growing tomatoes in buckets.

Her method was to ask for free used buckets from the local Walmart bakery, then drill a few drainage holes in them a couple of inches from the bottom. She would then fill the bottom with gravel and fill the remainder of the bucket with potting soil up to an inch from the rim of the bucket, then plant her tomatoes.

We decided to do the same thing. It was fun, and it meant we didn't have to get out the pickaxe to build our garden. Instead, we'd just put a bunch of buckets in rows and completely bypass the clay.

In fact, we decided to improve on her idea. Instead of buying potting soil, we had a guy deliver a load of soil, which he told us was good, rich dirt from the river bottom. It was much cheaper than buying bagged soil. We were so smart. He arrived with a load and dumped it in the backyard. It was orange, and looked a lot like our native clay, except it was looser and drier.

Before he arrived, we had scrounged lots of buckets from every place we could find them, checking bakeries and asking friends to save them for us.

We also got some gravel from somewhere, then started filling the bottom of the buckets with it, following it with our boutique river bottom soil.

We started planting and watered the bucket gardens well. It was a satisfying day.

Then the soil started to dry up and we realized our river bottom soil looked suspiciously like... wait... yes... oh no...

It was clay. It was clay that was almost exactly like the clay in our yard. In the buckets it rapidly settled into hard, poorly-draining Tennessee clay. Our high-class soil was a bust.

At that point, I was very annoyed with the entire project. We grew some plants in those buckets but they didn't do all that great. Later, we lived in a different house and did deep mulching on top of the hard clay, building beds right in the ground. That worked much better. When we moved back to Florida, I tried the bucket gardening trick again with much better luck because I got some soil that actually drained. My sister Rachel also made some 5-gallon bucket gardens with her family and grew fresh herbs, salad greens and tomatoes on the balcony of her second-floor apartment with great success. That was also in potting soil, not in imaginary top soil that turned out to be clay.

When you're putting plants into containers, the soil really matters. You often cannot just use regular dirt from the ground, as it gets compacted and airless over time. There's a reason potting mix was invented!

Incidentally, if you don't want to spend money on potting mix, you can make your own. Let's take an aside here and I'll share.

How To Make Homemade Potting Soil

First, you'll need a place to work. I like to spread a tarp on the grass and use that as my mixing area, but you can work on any solid surface. A tarp is easy to roll back and forth to help you mix, but making potting soil isn't rocket science and you can really do it anywhere. A driveway or patio works great.

Once you have your work space, gather your materials. My potting soil recipe has three main ingredients:

1. Rotten Wood

Fresh wood chips will eat up a lot of the nitrogen in your potting soil mix and can cause your plants to struggle. Rotten wood doesn't cause that issue, plus it holds moisture and provides a loose and airy texture to the mix. Leaving a pile of brush and logs in a corner of your property to rot over time will give you a ready source of rotten wood.

If you haven't started doing that yet, just go for a walk in the woods and get a nice sack of fluffy, crumbly wood and drag it home. If you can't find rotten wood, you can also use leaf mold. We have gone into the woods and dug up the rotten layer of humus beneath the leaves and used it just fine. Rotten pine bark and needles work well too.

2. Aged or Dried Cow Manure

When I first started making this recipe, I gathered manure from my neighbor's cows and left it on a piece of galvanized roofing metal in the sun to age for a few weeks, as fresh cow manure is too "hot."

You can also just pile it up in a heap somewhere and let it rot down for a few months. That provides you with a nutritious, organic-matter-rich pile of good stuff for your homemade potting soil.

We've also found that dried cow patties work fine from the field. We own our own cows now and have the luxury of being able to gather well-dried patties for home-made potting soil mixes.

NOTE: Manure in the United States is often contaminated with long-term herbicides that will destroy your garden and your potted plants.

I have to put that warning in every one of my books. Gardeners keep getting hit with herbicide-contaminated manure, hay and compost, and I don't want to be responsible for any lost gardens. In short: if a cow grazes on land sprayed with these new herbicides—in particular Aminopyralid—that kill broad-leaf weeds without hurting the grass; OR, if a cow eats purchased hay from land sprayed with these toxins, the manure of that animal will often contain the poison. Even after being digested and composted, the toxin persists, and it will kill your garden. I've heard reports of gardens hurt by purchased garden soil, compost, manure, hay, bagged manure from a big box store and more. I don't trust mushroom compost either. It's all suspect now, because the supply line is a complicated thing, and these toxins are now being sprayed everywhere. Don't get hit.

But, let's get back to manure. I wanted manure for our gardens and potting soil mixes so much that we bought cows, so we no longer have to go hunt manure from our neighbors' herd. Interestingly, on YouTube, The Vedic Way uses just cow manure for a potting mix. As he states:

> How can I make perfect soil? Here's an overview. First you have to collect grass leaves and organic material as much as you can. Then you have to find a way to shred it into small-sized particles. At the same time you have to remove rocks or hard-to-break items and then you have to destroy the unwanted bacteria and unwanted seeds—usually done with heat.
>
> You have to inoculate with beneficial bacteria so that the whole decomposition process starts, and while it's happening you have to maintain a warm temperature all along. Then you have to wait for several months or a year until the beneficial bacteria take over, and during this whole period you have to avoid rainwater so that nutrients are not lost, and then you simply have to repeat this process many, many times to continuously feed your plants.
>
> Sounds like fun!
>
> There are several methods to accomplish this. One is with man-made machinery. You have to buy lawn mowers, mechanical sifters, shredders, composting tanks, bins, tarps, etc. Too expensive!
>
> Then there is the traditional compost pile. It is cheap but it takes a lot of work and you have to wait a long time, and all along you have to worry about rain water protection.

It just takes too much time. Others try to avoid all this work and waiting by simply buying fertilizer from the store. The problem is, it's not alive, it's not scalable, it's too expensive, and it's not homemade, so you can't do it at home! It's just too complicated.

So what is the Vedic way of making perfect soil? The cow: the perfect soil generator! She collects and shreds huge amounts of organic matter, she inoculates with beneficial bacteria within her body, and she automatically filters rocks and bigger particles to generate antiseptic seedless single units of perfect soil.

What's the procedure? First you have to collect the cow dung. Then you have to dry it on a wall for three days. Then you have to crush it when dry. And then automatically you'll have all the qualities of the perfect soil available for your gardening. Full of life, antiseptic, airy, soft, good drainage, full of nutrients, very fresh smell, good water retention, and no unwanted seeds. Then you can actually start your gardening projects successfully every single time.

There are innumerable benefits of having a cow. They are movable, easy to maintain, they are gentle, peaceful, you can get perfect soil very quickly, they reproduce to increase the output, and they will work every day of the year nonstop. As an extra gift you get milk, yogurt, and butter etcetera.[3]

Envisioning the cow as the perfect soil-creation machine is brilliant, and experimenting with one-ingredient cow manure potting soil is on our list of future experiments. Right now, however, we just use it as a portion of the mix.

3. Sifted Soil/Grit

To fill in the last bit of my potting soil mixes, we try to find some gritty soil or sand. We've sifted soil from our chicken run for this, as the extra life from their manuring and the scraps they dig into the soil is good for plant growth. We've also used construction sand or sifted grit from a creek bed. We've also just added good garden soil, old potting soil mix from expired plants and even rinsed beach sand.

Mix It All Up

Now all you need to do is get mixing.

Smash the rotten wood into smaller chunks, break up the cow patties, and pour in the grit. We use one part rotten wood, one part aged manure and one part grit/soil in our potting soil recipe, but don't overthink it. If it looks loose and feels good, the plants will be happy. And you can just make this mix without sand, if you like. It's lighter that way.

We often leave some big chunks of wood in our homemade potting soil. The potted plants seem to like them and they act as moisture reservoirs while keeping the soil loose.

If you need a finer homemade potting soil for starting seeds, just crush the mix finer or run a coarser mix through some hardware cloth to sift it.

Alternate Ingredients for Homemade Potting Soil

If you don't have cow manure, try goat or rabbit manure. Both work quite well. Homemade compost is also excellent, though we never seem to have enough for everything we want to do.

Don't have grit/sand available? Vermiculite or perlite both work nicely, though you have to buy them. Or drop the sand altogether, as mentioned before.

Rotten wood can be replaced with peat moss or coconut coir. We prefer the coir as it seems to repel water less. You can also use leaf mould. Sift it out in the local forest – it's wonderful.

Along with these ingredients, we've also added a little bit of ashes, plenty of crushed charcoal that's been soaked for a week in a fertilizer solution, coffee grounds, old potting soil, peanut shells and even moldy cocoa nibs.

When I ran my nursery business I often stretched my potting soil budget by mixing purchased soil with rotten wood chips I got from a local tree company and set aside for years to break down.

You can also build great big compost piles, then pot up plants in the compost.

Just keep your homemade potting soil loose and fluffy with a good mix of ingredients and your plants will do great.

Some sands and grits can be too dense or fine to add, so a really easy potting soil mix—if you have the ingredients—

is just to mix pine bark fines with compost, with about three parts pine bark to one part compost.

Gardening in Barrels

Old whiskey barrels can be cut in half the short way or the long way to make raised beds. They are often pricey, but lend a lot of charm to the garden. You can't grow a ton of food in one because they're not that big, but they work nicely on porches and patios, and for small herb gardens. I have a friend with a distillery who gave me some of his old barrels to use for planters. They're sitting on my driveway right now, because I'm writing this book instead of gardening. My plan is to put them on my porch and use them for growing citrus trees that will benefit from being out of the brunt of the frosts in my yard. I'll plant calamondins, key limes, kumquats, lemons and other small citrus and keep them as little bushes we can harvest through the winter months, and perhaps cart into the house during long cold snaps. The half-barrel planters really look classy. I've never bought them before because they're too expensive, but I'm really happy to have some for free.

Plastic barrels can also be used as planters/raised beds; however, I have found that they tend to warp when cut and need to be packed to the top with soil so they don't get a weird shape in the sun. Years ago my friend Curtiss made a really cool worm bin/garden for me out of a 55-gallon blue barrel. It featured a big piece of PVC piping down the center from the top where you could stuff food scraps to feed worms, plus about 40 holes in the sides of the barrel for planting small plants, like lettuces and strawberries.

This design is really neat, but I put it in my garden and it fell over in a rainstorm, smashing the plants on the downward side. That was a total user error, though. It would have been just fine on a patio. I made some similar gardens without the legs and the PVC center just by cutting slits in a plastic barrel and opening and bending them out with a heat gun and a wine bottle forced into the gap. In order to save on potting soil, I crammed the barrel with straw and only filled the holes and the open top with planting mix. This was a mistake. Within a month or so, the straw started to sink and it pulled my transplants down into the holes. If I did it again, I would make a bigger batch of potting soil or perhaps use sand to fill out the extra space.

Cinderblocks

We've made multiple beds with cinderblocks. My friend Allan the Beekeeper told me about a demolition site where piles of cinderblocks lay for the taking. We loaded up a truck and a trailer and brought some to his place and some to my place. He used his for supporting beehives, I used mine to build some raised garden beds.

We also used cinderblock borders on the first two prototype Grocery Row Gardens back in 2014. In the beds we planted multiple raspberry varieties, along with some herbs, a perennial marigold, cutleaf coneflowers, and Lion's ear plants for the pollinators. In a second, longer bed, we had a large moringa tree, lemon balm, variegated shell ginger, turmeric, chayote squash and a Red Angel pomegranate tree with a birdhouse hanging from it.

After building these beds, I later read that cinderblocks may contain heavy metals.

As Jessica W. reports at OffTheGridNews:

> Cement blocks are made with Portland cement and aggregates. They are heavier and costlier on average, while cinder blocks are made with Portland cement and fly ash, a byproduct of the coal industry, and they are lighter in weight and most often cheaper to purchase.
>
> The addition of fly ash to the Portland cement is the cause of concern. Fly ash is a byproduct of coal-burning electric plants. The ash is trapped and collected, then used as a partial substitute for Portland cement. While it is true that this process creates what is now considered a green building material, questions remain about how safe fly ash truly is. The coal itself contains many heavy metals and other substances known to be toxic. A considerable amount of these metals and substances remain in the ash and are subsequently found in the cinder blocks that are created from it.
>
> Garden beds, framed with cinder block, may be fine for flowers and other nonedible plants, but be wary of using them to frame gardens that will be home to edible

plants and medicinal herbs. There is the potential for toxic materials to leach from the cinder blocks into the soil. These materials have been known to affect cognitive ability, cause nervous disorders, contribute to increased cancer risks and have given rise to many general health complaints.[4]

Oh come on... is everything toxic now? I am so disappointed. I love cinderblocks. AND NOW EVEN THEY ARE TRYING TO KILL US!

Though, who really knows without a test?

Other reports say that they don't leach much, or that they leach some lime which can raise pH. Perhaps you could paint them with acrylic paint to stop the leaching—or just figure you're gonna die some day anyhow. We don't currently have any cinderblock beds, but they don't worry us too much.

Horse Troughs

Who doesn't love artsy-looking galvanized horse trough gardens, overflowing with beautiful vegetables? You can put a bunch of rotten wood in the bottom of a horse trough or other deep raised bed to fill up the first foot or so of space, then top off with potting soil so you don't have to buy a ton of soil. The main problem with using horse troughs as gardens is the price! At the writing of this book, the CountyLine "300 gal Oval Galvanized Stock Tank 3 ft x 8 ft x 2 ft" at Tractor Supply is $329.

Maybe when I'm rich enough to own a new Kubota tractor, I'll also be rich enough to get some $329 gardens for the porch.

Oh, who am I kidding? If I had money like that, I would just spend it on more fruit trees. Or maybe I would buy a FULL barrel of whiskey, then drink the whiskey, then cut the barrel in half to make two more planters for my front porch citrus collection. That sounds like a plan. Better than buying horse troughs. Though if you have a horse trough, it really does make a great garden.

I once went to the dump with my friend Sam to drop off some trash. While we were throwing junk out of his trailer, we spotted a good-looking horse trough sitting in the piles of trash and I convinced him to load it onto his trailer.

We finished off-loading our trash and headed down the hill. Then, suddenly, the gates closed in front of us and we were stopped by the trash police (I guess that's what you'd call them) for "stealing" that horse trough. Much to Sam's embarrassment, we had to go back up the hill of trash and throw it back into the pile. How stupid is that? It was a perfectly good trough that was being thrown away. It was literally in a garbage pile. And they wouldn't let us take it, even though we'd dumped a ton of other trash and paid for the privilege.

See, that would have been a great garden, since it would have been free. But no... BIG HORSE TROUGH apparently controls the dumps and wants us to pay full price.

Old Fridges and Freezers

You can make a really simple raised bed garden from an old fridge or freezer. However, there are all kinds of weird chemicals in appliances so it's not the best raised bed idea for truly crunchy gardeners. Also, I heard that if you release the refrigerant from a fridge improperly, you're apparently on the hook for major fines from the EPA, because it destroys the ozone layer and melts the ice caps and kills polar bears and stuff, so definitely don't do that. However, if you do release coolant on accident, while you're, say, hacking holes in bottom of a chest freezer, you really need to make sure to plant a few trees or recycle a sofa or something to balance it out. Maybe two sofas, especially if you're getting rid of low-carbon sofas. Actually, better throw in three sofas, since you almost certainly have a neighbor who isn't as green as you. That's it, though. All you have to do to cancel out the sin of hacking through a refrigerant line is to recycle three sofas as penance, and *absolvo te*, you're good.

We had a great worm bin in an old fridge once. Another time we planted an herb garden in a defunct chest freezer. I knocked a few holes in the bottom of the freezer and definitely did not puncture any coolant lines while doing so, then put the freezer up on bricks and loaded the interior with rotten wood and leaves, before topping off with homemade potting soil and then planting herb transplants. It was very Pinterest-postable.

Pressure-Treated Wood

Wood beds are easy to make, but cheap wood rots... except for pressure-treated wood! That stuff lasts for years and we've used it in multiple raised beds. Generally we use 2x6 pressure treated pine. Older pressure-treated wood contained arsenic, yet the new stuff does not. Instead, it's treated with ACQ, AKA Alkaline copper quaternary. According to Iowa State:

> This wood preservative has been available since the 1990s but its use increased after CCA was removed from the market. Today, it is the most widely used wood preservative for residential applications. ACQ is both a fungicide and an insecticide. Water-based preservatives like ACQ leave a dry, paintable surface.
>
> There are multiple variations of ACQ: ACQ-B is ammonium copper quaternary formulation; ACQ-C is formulated with ammonia or amine and a quaternary compound; and ACQ-D is an amine copper quaternary formulation. ACQ is registered for use on lumber, timbers, landscape ties, fence posts, building and utility poles, land, freshwater and marine pilings, sea walls, decking, wood shingles, and other wood structures.
>
> ACQ has relatively low risks, based on its components of copper oxide and quaternary ammonium compounds. Research (wipe testing) was conducted to determine the amount of chemical a person could contact dermally and then put in their mouth. Results showed that ACQ-treated wood is essentially non-toxic by normal dermal and oral exposures. Another study showed that copper

did leach out of treated railroad ties following destructive sampling (cutting or grinding), but this research was done to determine if the ties would constitute a hazard when disposed.[5]

Of course, just because something is considered safe or "low-risk," it doesn't mean it's a great idea to use it. We had a few pressure-treated raised beds we put in for herbs last year, then we changed out minds and pulled them out. Those pressure-treated 4' x 8' beds were moved to our plant nursery and filled with sand for propagating seeds and cuttings. If you don't want to bother with pressure-treated wood, just cut some logs and use those for the sides. We've done that in the past and it has some advantages over pressure-treated wood.

First, log beds are free, as you can usually find large tree limbs or small trunks that will work. Giant trunks will work, of course, but the logistics of moving and placing them can be considerable. Second, as the logs rot down slowly into the ground they feed the soil and provide habitat for worms and beetles. Third, log beds are chemical-free. The down side is they may harbor termites, yet termites do create nice soil over time. After a few years you may have to replace the logs, of course, but at least you haven't left industrial chemicals in your garden.

To keep logs in place you can buy large screws and make notches in out of the corners with a sawsall or chainsaw, then screw them together—or you can just hammer some stakes (which can be made from branches) around the edges as needed to hold them in place.

As we've become more aware of the toxicity of the industrial world, from BPAs to phthalates, and preservatives to heavy metals, we've become more and more leery of "low-risk" toxins. We're constantly bombarded with a huge range of chemicals and we probably shouldn't add more if we can help it—especially when trying to garden organically. First cinder blocks... now pressure-treated...

And speaking of toxic gardening, my Dad helped me build my first garden when I was six. He built it from four discarded railroad ties in an 8' x 8' rectangle. I'm sure they contained creosote and probably arsenic and who knows what else. Honestly, I'll be lucky to live long enough to finish writing this book.

Stones and Bottles

In Tennessee we had plenty of stones we could use to build beds. They worked great when stacked and fit as needed and had a nice rustic look. It's time-consuming to build from stone but they last forever. If you have an abundant source of rock and are good at masonry, you can really make beautiful, tall raised beds. We also built some beds by knocking old wine bottles into the ground, neck-first. That worked okay except for the occasional broken bottle; however, it made us look like winos.

But... do we need all these things? These bordered, raised beds and container gardens? They may be useful in some situations—and they certainly can grow you plenty of food—but they aren't the end-all. What if we went even simpler?

Chapter 3

Dejunking Your Garden

We'll start with what may be the simplest of all gardening systems: the row garden.

Though our food forest projects and Grocery Row Gardens feature a complex (though not elaborately planned) mix of species, our vegetable gardens—especially on new land—are often simple row gardens designed for the easy and rapid production of produce for the table.

Single-Row Gardening

When you need to grow food fast, simple and time-tested gardening methods are the way to go. Just because single-row gardening is no longer as common as raised beds and intensive gardening does not mean it isn't a great method.☐

For market gardening and survival gardening, it's hard to beat the ease and simplicity of this tried-and-true method. In a very short period of time and with limited resources you can quickly produce an abundance of food.

Our row gardens are planted in single rows with 3' spacing between rows, which allows us to garden with little to no irrigation as well as use very little fertilizer. It also makes the entire garden exceptionally easy to weed, especially with a wheel hoe.

As The Fishing Hole wrote in the comments one of our videos:

> I just about gave up on gardening a few years ago because of YouTube gardening videos.
>
> I'm sitting on 25 acres of land, but I had my poor husband out building raised beds. I was crawling around on the ground laying down plastic weed suppressing fabric and trying to figure out how to get everything to grow vertically. I bought expensive bags of worm castings and lost an entire potato crop to potato bugs, which I was trying to kill with dish soap. I watched this woman planting in her raised beds while reciting poetry and teaching me how to use a black light at night to find and squish horn worms on tomatoes.
>
> I had planted enough seeds for a zillion acres of farm land, and I ended up with like four tomatoes, six beautiful asparagus spears and a gigantic parsley bush (which I never watered, weeded, or looked at). No food, no fun, and no poetry.
>
> Then I watched your videos, and I thought, "Hey, I'll just throw some seeds out, try to weed, and possibly fertilize with diluted urine." I'm STILL digging potatoes that I forgot I planted, sweet potatoes that I never weeded, and tons of other food, some of which we ate tonight. No kidding, you are a voice crying out in the wilderness, and

DEJUNKING YOUR GARDEN

you saved me from boutique gardening. And thank you for not caving to trends. Grow on, my brother!!!!

Keep it simple!

When you have so-so soil, some extra space, no permanent irrigation and need food fast, single-row gardens are excellent.

As Steve Solomon wrote to me after seeing one of my videos on single-row gardening:

> Gardening without (much) irrigation only works well in single rows well spaced. Your soil has very little capacity to hold moisture, yet it went for weeks without watering. Had you used wider in-the-row spacing it could have gone twice as long without watering.

Wide spacing works. The modern intensive gardening movement is, like many other modern movements, not nearly as good as advertised.

And as for raised beds, sure—they have benefits! But here's the truth: you don't need boundaries on your beds to make raised beds. All you need is a mound of soil.

Just going through that big list of raised bed ideas reminds me how refreshing it is to dump the junk and just work with the soil.

Forget making a trip to Home Depot or Lowe's to get lumber, then spending a few hours measuring and cutting and nailing and placing beds. And don't get sold ready-made raised bed kits. I get emails for those things regularly. If you know me, you know I don't really take sponsors—though it doesn't stop companies from trying. Like this email I received recently:

> Hi David,
>
> I'm the Sales Team Leader at ———. We are big fans of your channel, and I really love your videos. They're quite valuable and encouraging.
>
> We're looking for creators like you, who align with our core values of "To grow a natural, healthy, eco-friendly and low-carbon garden" who would be willing to create Youtube video and share valuable gardening contents.
>
> You can read a little more background on our brand here:... We're a company mainly providing a range of Zn-Al-Mg metal garden beds for worldwide customers.
>
> Because of your interest and expertise in gardening, we think you would be perfect! We would like to give you free metal raised garden beds to help you take some videos and pictures on your channel. Certainly, we would love to negotiate with you if you have other requirements.
>
> We're reaching out because we believe you are an excellent fit for our brand. If it sounds interesting, please tell us when you are available for a follow-up chat.
>
> Emma
> Sales Team Leader

I said no, of course, as I do to pretty much every company that writes. I don't want more stuff. And you don't need Zn-Al-Mg beds. Or those plastic pre-made kits Walmart sells.

Stop filling your life with junk. You don't even need to buy cinder blocks. Or scrounge for old appliances or rocks. And buying cedar for your garden beds is roughly equivalent to burning stacks of $100 bills to keep warm.

It's expensive. And you also need to deal with building the beds. Sure, build bordered raised beds if you like—especially if you need to grow on a concrete driveway or in a vole-infested location—though most of the time, you don't need them.

Most of the time, we just use a modified version of the easy raised-bed design recommended by John Jeavons in his book *How to Grow More Vegetables*. No borders, just a nice section of well-dug earth which you DON'T step on after digging. That ground will stay loose for a long time. We've planted on year-old double-dug beds and they were still nice and loose.

Jeavons recommends double-digging 5-foot-wide beds with a fork and a spade. This system works well, but there are a few things we changed for our own gardening. We prefer wide spacing to tight spacing, especially in situations where we need to haul water. We've also stopped re-digging beds, for the most part; instead, we just add compost from the top and let plant roots and worms keep the soil loose. Give them some room and they'll compete less. Tighter spacing creates a need for more water and much higher soil fertility. Widely spaced plants are better at taking care of themselves.

The theory with 5-foot wide beds is that they create a microclimate as the plants grow together and the leaves touch. I don't know about that as I haven't tested it; 4-foot beds have worked fine for me. Even 3-foot beds are great. 5-foot beds are too much to reach over. They just feel clunky.

Instead of double digging with a spade and fork, we now do most of our digging with a Meadow Creature broadfork, a triangular hoe we got from Easy Digging, and a landscape rake. The broadfork doesn't break ground as thoroughly as a fork and spade, but you can go a lot faster and cover much larger gardens without breaking your back. It's a much easier tool to use and is rather like rowing. It feels good to broadfork—much more so than digging with a spade. Or, of course, you can have a friend with a tractor till the area for you, or just rent a tiller and tear up a space, then start shaping your beds.

Once I have my bed loosened, I shape it up with the triangular hoe. Then we use a rake to level the seedbed. In between beds, I like 3 foot paths when I grow larger crops. Less than that and you're always crowded. Our old homestead had beds with less than 2 feet between beds, and I was growing everything. It was tight!

Sure, you save on space, but it's harder to work and feels claustrophobic. Spread out!

A simple 4 foot x 8 foot raised bed mound like these can be built in perhaps a half hour in sandy soil, and a couple of hours in clay.

The plants love these beds just as much as beds with borders. Why make cedar raised beds or square-foot garden beds with pressure-treated lumber when you can just dig mounded beds like these? It's so easy—and we find these easy raised beds are better when it comes to weeding, as well. There's no wood for the weeds to work themselves in around.

If you're looking to try something new in your spring garden and haven't built this style of mounded bed before, give it a try. This is about the easiest garden you can make, and it's free. There's no need to spend money on borders anymore. Just make neat mound gardens and plant them up. The vegetables will make them beautiful.

In the Caribbean, farmer James "Mike" Thomas showed me how to make mounded beds for yams, cassava and other root crops with just a sharp digging hoe with a handle from a sturdy wild coffee branch. He'd start by cropping the grass down to the ground with a machete, and then dig a trench with the hoe, chopping and pulling soil up into a mound, then repeating the process by hacking soil from the next strip down into the trench. This had the effect of loosening the soil a foot or so deep, and then the mound on top of the trench went even higher up by a foot and a half or so. The mounds were perhaps 18" tall with about 18" in between them for a walking space. This allowed roots to go deep, and it also kept the crops from flooding in torrential rains. The mounds were made perpendicular to the slope of a hill to reduce erosion, and were dug after the first few rains of the rainy season when the soil had been softened by moisture.

If you don't have issues with flooding and are on flat ground, you can also just do single-row gardening and skip the mounds altogether, as I cover in the beginning of the chapter.

That is truly minimalist! They're super easy to weed with a hoe. If you have larger gardens, a wheel hoe is even better—but we'll talk about weeding a little later on.

My friend Noah Sanders organized the "well-watered garden" project. This style of gardening doesn't require any tilling at all. As he relates in *The Well-Watered Garden Handbook*:

> In order to prepare for planting our vegetable crops, we must first remove the existing plants (weeds). Just like in the Parable of the Sower the Jesus told, weeds will grow up and choke our crops, robbing them of water, nutrients and sunlight. Typically, it is when we see a field of weeds that we first consider grabbing a tiller or hoe. But in order to reflect the wisdom of God's design in creation, we are going to use one of several methods that will allow us to remove the weeds with minimal soil disturbance. After using your string to connect the four corner stakes of your plot and defining the area you need to weed you have three options:
>
> Option #1: Cut off weeds at ground level using a hoe or shovel. No digging! This method is quick, works well with thick grass and sod, and is best done when the soil is dry. Remove the weeds and let them dry in the sun to use for mulch or making compost.
>
> Option #2: Pull weeds by hand, shaking dirt off the roots back on the garden. This method is best for large, clumpy weeds and works best when the soil is moist. Remove the weeds and let them dry spread out in a thin layer to use later for mulch or making compost.

Option #3: Use a tarp or other material to smother the grass and weeds within your plot. If the grass or weeds are tall mow or trample them down. Before applying the tarp thoroughly soak the plants and soil to help activate the microbes that will break down the material while they are covered up. Use rocks, boards, or heavy sticks to securely weight down edges of the tarp or plastic so it doesn't blow away. A few weeks in the summer will be enough to kill and break down the weeds. You can either rake off or leave the leftover residue, depending on how broken down it is when you go to lay off your beds.

The layout is similar to how we build our gardens, though the pathways are much narrower, as it is a system focused on annual crops, rather than big perennials.

Each bed will be allocated 42 inches (3.5 ft) for the growing area and 18 inches (1.5 ft) for paths. This means that each bed/path combo will be 5 feet wide, with all four beds spanning the 20' plot width. In order to center the beds, we will have two 9-inch border paths and three, 18-inch central paths. Use your tape measure to locate and install the corner stakes on each end. (Tip: You can make a marker string/rope cut to 20' with loops on the end and beads glued where the bed corners should be. One or two of these can be used to locate your bed corners without having to leave your stakes in the ground as a tripping hazard. A steel rod or rebar hammered flush with the ground at the four corners of your plot will allow you to locate them in the future and lay-off your plot in the same place each time.) Mark off the paths with string.

The beds themselves are not tilled at all! The weeds are just removed. And then you:

> ...use a shovel or hoe to remove one to two inches of soil from the paths and add it evenly to the beds on either side. If you are in a drier climate raise your beds only a little. If you are in a wetter climate raise them more. You are not digging in your beds at all. You are only adding soil from the path to them. This will ensure that the lowest parts of your WWG are the paths so excess water drains away from your plants.

We had the pleasure of assisting with the creation of two "Well-Watered Gardens" at Noah's homestead during the 2022 and 2023 *Redeeming the Dirt* conferences. We used sharp grub hoes to chop the weeds off just below ground level, then we raked them up and threw them aside to be composted, then we dug out the paths and threw that loose topsoil on top of the beds and raked them even. In the well-watered garden, you never leave the soil bare, so as a final covering, the paths were filled with wood chips and the planting beds were mulched with organic hay or straw. To plant them, you simply pull back the mulch and uncover the soil beneath and pop in your seeds or transplants. It's very easy, and you don't have to do much digging at all compared to broad-forking, tilling, or double-digging with a fork and spade. You can learn more about the well-watered garden project by visiting wellwateredgardenproject.org

The draw to buy stuff to fill your garden is real, whether it's whiskey barrels or cedar garden beds, huge terracotta pots or a horse trough. Sometimes buying or repurposing something is just right for the space you're working with. I once saw an gigantic old sugar kettle used as a pond full of beautiful water lilies at an old English estate in the West Indies. It was the perfect thing in the perfect spot. Likewise, you might have a tiny patio that would be greatly improved by a single half-barrel garden overflowing with fragrant herbs and bright nasturtiums. If it brings you joy, and not just the fading dopamine rush of purchasing something, enjoy it.

There is also an appeal to reusing something free as a garden bed. There's a desire to save junk from the dump, to be clever and artsy, to say "see how much I saved on raised beds!" (Though I once saw an entire garden made from old appliances and bathtubs. You know what it looked like? It looked like a dump!)

An old-fashioned single row garden would have been much more beautiful than a bunch of ugly junk sprouting greenery.

Less is more.

You'll rarely see a garden more beautiful than one with simple beds with clean lines and happy vegetables growing on top. A birdhouse or a bamboo trellis or a little white picket fence and gate might enhance the space, but even without decor it's beautiful just because of its clean functionality and the happy plants. There is a beauty in something that is useful for its purpose and that serves us daily.

In our gardens we usually use old washtubs and wicker baskets to carry produce because they are clean and functional and non-plastic. I have really come to hate plastic in the gardens. My garden is a place where I go to connect with nature and nature's Creator, and to bring in beautiful produce for my family. In my mind a ripe tomato or a watermelon, or a basket of beets or a handful of berries is made even more beautiful because of its humble origins in the soil. A persimmon or a bundle of asparagus is more beautiful than a garden gazing globe, as living fireflies on a dark night are more lovely than a chintzy spray of garden LED lights from a sweatshop in China.

There are two threads running through this chapter; the practical and the beautiful. It may be practical to garden in an old freezer, but it's not beautiful. A tall cedar garden bed may be beautiful but not practical. Yet the practical and the beautiful can combine in a simple raised bed garden overflowing with red and green cabbages, or a little corner bed beside the house with an espaliered apple tree.

Your primary goal is to grow food to feed the body, but in doing so you can also feed the soul. We were made to be gardeners, and we were made from the soil. Before jumping into container gardens or being sold complex solutions, learn to work with the soil you have. Don't give up right away and jump to container gardens and buying in materials. In doing so, also don't forget beauty—especially the beauty in something simple, clean and productive.

Why not de-junk your garden and let your happy plants be your main focus? It's a goal, at least. There are places for raised beds, but they aren't the final solution for everything. Perhaps a handicapped-accessible bed may be what you need to grow food; or, you may only have a small piece of concrete as a garden, and a horse trough might be the answer—but, really, most of the time we can make due with just the soil the Lord gave us, and there is a real joy in the simplicity and frugality of growing that way. It's also redemptive, in that you're taking unproductive ground and improving it.

No purchases required!

Chapter 4

Free Fertilizer

Feeding your garden doesn't have to be that difficult. There's a scene in the film *The Big Short* where two young stock traders are at the off-grid cabin of an old iconoclastic trader who is helping them break in to the system. The young guys are eating a salad from the man's garden, and the fellow is ranting about the food system, and says something like, "You can grow a great garden with nothing but urine and wood ashes," which just about causes his guests to spit out their food.

It's true, though. If you really needed to grow a garden and didn't have any fertilizer, you could just dilute urine and water the garden with it. About 6–10 parts water to 1 part urine is perfect.

However, that's pretty out there for many of us. And it will make your dinner guests get weirded out. And come on, it's gross. Sure, you'll live, but still.

So let's look at other free fertilizers we can use to feed our minimalist garden.

Dave's Fetid Swamp Water

Okay, this one is also a big gross. So let's get the most divisive fertilizer out of the way first. "Dave's Fetid Swamp Water," as I call it, is one of the easiest ways to feed the garden. The idea is simple: just take a wide range of decomposable materials and throw them into the bottom of a barrel, then cover with water and let the concoction rot down for a few weeks or months, then ladle it out as a liquid garden fertilizer.

You can use a bit of chicken manure, some comfrey leaves, weeds, grass, some cow patties, kitchen scraps, seaweed, ashes, kudzu vines, nettles, fish guts, and many other ingredients. We just use what we currently have available. Over time, these materials rot down into a liquid nutrient suspension that can revitalize a struggling garden.

The problem is that this method can also kill your garden, especially if you make a batch that is too strong. Determining dosages is not all that easy. I've found that a shovelful or two of chicken manure and a bunch of weeds in 55 gallons of water is fine for direct application, but people also write me and tell me they've turned their plant leaves yellow when they applied straight fetid swamp water. Without knowing what originally went in their barrels, I can't determine what went wrong. Especially when many other people write to tell me that their swamp water worked miracles in the garden, rejuvenating struggling plants and turning a wasteland into a garden of Eden.

The safest thing to do when using swamp water is to dilute the first round and see what happens when you water with it. If plants start to turn yellow, it's still too hot. If nothing happens, then dilute it less or try using it straight. If plants green up on the first application and look happy, you have probably found the sweet spot. But each batch will vary, depending on what you have available.

We've used mimosa leaves and chicken guts, cow manure and old kefir, coffee grounds and bones, rotten eggs and weeds, chunks of moringa trees... it's always a different mix. And I'm not the type to make recipes, either. And even if I did, the relative amount of salts and nitrogen and fermentation products are going to change during the year as the composition of ingredients and the weather changes. Grass clippings in the spring don't have the same nitrogen content as grass clippings in the fall, for instance. If you make DFSW, just remember that though it's a fantastic way to make fertilizer, it's more of an art than a science.

Another objection to swamp water is the incredible smell it creates. The anaerobic fermentation of material unleashes some absolutely righteous aromas. The good news is that batches that sit for longer periods often lose a lot of their horrific odor. When a batch gets to six months or so, it may even smell good. I had one batch that reminded me of soy sauce. My guess is that the volatile compounds that may be harsher on plants will also mellow with further fermentation. We need to do more experimentation, but the Korean Natural

Farmers have said that it is better for the garden when well-aged, so keep that in mind.

We have found that about two weeks of rot time is good enough to break down the original materials and make fetid swamp water in warm weather. Sometimes we add more stuff to the mix and let it rot in, other times we dump the barrel out and start over – usually when mosquitoes move in because we accidentally left the barrel uncovered.

One barrel is usually good enough to feed maybe 2,000 square feet of crops. We usually don't bother diluting with corn and bananas, since they're really hungry, so they take more. If we diluted further and/or started with a "hotter" barrel, i.e., more manure or nitrogenous materials, we might manage 5,000 square feet.

There's not a lot of testable or reproducible science in the swamp water method since inputs vary so much. Sometimes you have chicken manure to use, sometimes not. Sometimes weeds. Sometimes nitrogen fixers and moringa. Sometimes kitchen scraps. Sometimes rotten fish. It's hard to figure out exact dosages. I've never burned anything with it, though, so so far so good. I just "feel" it, like some sort of hippy.

Some have asked me about weed seeds in swamp water. Weed seeds often decay, but not always. It depends on the species. The longer they sit in the water, however, the less likely they are to be a problem. Weed seeds might survive for a few days or a week or two, but are much less likely to still be viable after a month or more. If you are concerned about spreading a particular weed, skip adding it when in seed. I rarely add seedy material, since I usually start using my swamp water within just a few weeks of making it.

Making fetid swamp water is an easy way to feed the garden, and it's hard to screw it up. If it has bugs in it or mold in it or mosquito larvae or whatever – don't worry about it. The plants won't care, and insect larvae are just more food for the soil.

Coffee Grounds

A woman wrote recently and said:

> I read an article from someone claiming that coffee grounds kill earthworms — the leftover caffeine does it. She had photos of the dead worms. I know coffee grounds are popular for compost. People even go to coffee shops to lug away plastic bags of their spent grounds. But are they bad for microbes and worms?

Anything that dies after drinking God's Gift of coffee deserves to die.

That said, we add coffee grounds to our worm bins, often in huge quantities, and they have not gone to the big compost pile in the sky. These are *Einsenia foetida*, AKA red wigglers, however, and are not the same worms in garden soil. Maybe coffee grounds will kill worms. Or maybe—even worse— there were pesticides in those coffee grounds.

Or maybe the coffee grounds were from the local Brethren Assembly. Brethren churches have the worst coffee I have ever tasted, other than the coffee that used to be brewed in an aluminum percolator in the upstairs office hallway at Coral Ridge Presbyterian Church. I do have a theory, however, that the worse the church coffee, the better the theology. The coffee at St. Stephen's Roman Catholic church in Pensacola is also rather poor. Perhaps the Presbyterians, Brethren and Catholics all need to fight it out—or maybe they can all gang up for a Holy War against the excellent coffee brewers at Calvary Chapel.

We have also used coffee grounds to feed the grass by just throwing the used grounds across the lawn. Coffee grounds are also a good food for roses, who particularly love the combination of a coffee filter full of grounds with a few tablespoons of Epsom salts.

All that said, we haven't tried to do a vegetable garden test with coffee-grounds infused soil next to soil without coffee grounds. We just *believe* coffee grounds are a decent fertilizer because the roses and grass did fine, so we throw them around. Trust the SCIENCE!

Lasagna Gardening

In the last chapter we talked about making raised beds by digging or tilling. But you could skip all that if you have enough organic material to make a "Lasagna Garden" instead.

FREE FERTILIZER

This method both feeds and builds soil while creating raised beds and producing healthy food fast.

Nature is a compost-generating machine. Every fall, leaves drift down from the tree canopy, blanketing the ground with organic matter. Over the following year, those leaves break down into rich humus that feeds plant roots, increases the water-holding capacity of the soil, harbors beneficial organisms, and softens hard ground.

Lasagna gardening does the same.

In 2019 we recorded a demonstration video where I built a lasagna garden from scratch, Patricia Lanza style. She wrote the original book *Lasagna Gardening*, which I greatly enjoyed and have put to good use for decades. In my demonstration, I layered a wide range of organic matter—ranging from seaweed to hay to water hyacinth plants—creating a quick, beautiful, and weed-free garden space.

Yet I didn't maintain that garden after we built it.

At this point, if I cared to defend myself, I could share with you how I built my demonstration garden on a piece of borrowed land and how we then moved to a new plot of land and how it was the dry season and how we didn't have irrigation and how...

But really, it didn't matter. I did the video on lasagna gardening just so I had a video for an online event. I made a few bucks, and then I abandoned it, like I abandoned my last three wives when they questioned my addiction to binge-buying rare yams on Etsy with the mortgage money.

Seriously, though—we've built plenty of lasagna gardening beds and they always work wonderfully, provided they are actually maintained a little.

Even when they aren't maintained, lasagna gardens do a great job of building the soil in a manner that mimics nature, with a few tweaks that make it even more productive than leaves falling on a forest floor. The "Back to Eden" garden works the same way. Lots and lots of organic matter is laid on top of untilled soil; then, over time, it rots down to give you some of the most amazing ground you've ever seen.

The bed I abandoned still made great soil! I revisited the spot a year after creating my demonstration video and dug up the area to see how it looked beneath the top layer of mulch. To my satisfaction, I found a perfect patch of compost, and some of the perennials I had planted were still alive.

We ended up getting about ten gallons of rich compost from that bed. The ground beneath the loose humus on top is also rich and could almost certainly support a wonderful vegetable garden without supplemental feeding, even with the layer on top gone.

Last year we decided to build another lasagna garden in an awful sand-pit grit garden area. We had similar results. Now that area is the best over there, and we got about three times the sweet potatoes from that space than we got from our non-lasagna beds.

Don't buy the tall tales about how you need complicated systems or bins or tumblers and constant turning and perfect ratios of carbon and nitrogen to build compost. It's not true. Throw organic matter on the ground and it will break down into lovely humus. If you have hard or poor soil, water the ground, throw down some cardboard, pile up organic matter, then get planting. It's easy to do and the results are excellent.

Lasagna gardening works best for small gardens, as all the materials required really take effort to acquire and use. It's both a gardening technique and a fertilization method, as the constant slow decay of materials over time perpetually feeds your crops.

Other Easy Ways to Feed the Garden

For the book *Florida Survival Gardening*, I created a big list of amendments you can use to easily feed your garden, including alfalfa, ammonia, animal carcasses, ashes, bat guano, biochar, blood meal, bone meal, borax, chemical fertilizers, chicken manure, comfrey leaves, compost, composted stable bedding, cottonseed meal, cow manure, crab meal, dog food, eggshells, epsom salts, fish fertilizer, goat manure, grass clippings, greensand, gypsum, horse manure, human hair, humanure, kelp meal, leaf mould, leguminous tree leaves, lime, milorganite, moringa, oak leaves, oyster shell, peanut hay, rabbit manure, rock dust, sea salt, seaweed, spanish moss, straw and hay, urea, urine, water hyacinth, weeds and wood chips.

Each amendment got its own write-up. And despite the huge list, I still forgot many things, like worm castings, azolla and duckweed, chicken run dirt, etc. etc. The ways to feed your garden are almost endless!

But what would the minimalist approach be? If you could use just one amendment to feed your garden, what would it be? My first choice would be homemade compost. My second choice would be cow manure. It adds humus and is a constantly renewing resource if you own a cow. But cow manure and homemade compost together are a really powerful combination.

If you don't have time to make compost, you could just go out to the woods with a shovel, a sifter and some buckets or a wheelbarrow and sift the rich leaf mould compost from beneath the trees. We've done that multiple times, getting good organic matter without having to plan ahead.

Yet one of many things I learned from Steve Solomon was the importance of micronutrients in the garden. He taught me that even an organic garden with happy-looking green plants may not give you all the micronutrients you need for maximum health. If your soil lacks certain minerals, your plants can't make them out of thin air. And if you compost from materials on your own land, you will just continue lacking those minerals in the finished product.

At least, according to current scientific knowledge. If the transmutation of elements is possible via biological processes, everything will get turned on its head.

We do know that microorganisms and fungi are ridiculously good at obtaining trace minerals for plants in a healthy soil, so you may not need to do a ton of amending to maintain good health.

With a good bit of effort, I managed to create Steve's Complete Organic Fertilizer (as most completely outlined in his recent book *Water-Wise Gardening*). As he writes:

> Repeated uses of COF gently move most soils into chemical balance and from the get-go it makes veggies grow fast and taste great. It entirely consists of substances that are allowed for use by organic certification agencies. Vegetables grow great when the soil is given only COF and small additions of compost.
>
> COF costs only a tiny fraction of the supermarket price of the vegetables it grows—if you buy the major ingredients in 50 pound bags. Farm/ranch suppliers are the most likely sources. If you should find COF ingredients at a garden shop they will almost inevitably be offered in small quantities at shockingly high prices per pound. If I were an urban gardener I would drive to a country store and stock up.
>
> A fertilizer that puts the highest nutritional content into the vegetables it grows must provide roughly equal amounts of nitrogen (N), phosphorus (P), and potassium (K, from kalium, its Latin name). It would also supply substantial amounts of calcium (Ca) and sulfur (S) and effective quantities of iodine, manganese, copper, zinc, molybdenum, boron, etc. I stress the word "effective" because a lab analysis of many prepared fertilizers (printed on the package at a garden center) may show all these elements are present but when the numbers are crunched it becomes

clear that the amounts are too small to make a nutritional difference. An ideal garden fertilizer would release most of its nutrients over a few months instead of in a few days. That way they don't wash out of the topsoil with the first excessive irrigation or heavy rain. It would be odorless, finely powdered, not burn leaves if a little got on them and would not poison plants or soil life if accidentally double-dosed. All this accurately describes COF.

It worked excellently, and the vegetables we harvested with from the test bed were rich in flavor and much larger than most all the other vegetables we grew. I'll leave it to Steve to share his final recipe, but it contains all the little stuff we overlook in our focus on nitrogen, phosphorus, and potassium. Elements like molybdenum, copper, manganese, boron and sulfur, which also perform essential functions in plants.

The problem was that obtaining and mixing all these elements was not a minimalist process. We currently have bins of esoteric materials behind an outbuilding in a series of labeled trash cans. My just "throw it on the ground!" method of composting outlined in *Compost Everything* is much more adapted to my gardening style. Steve's mix works like magic, especially in humus-rich soil, but it takes a lot of hunting for materials as well as measuring and mixing.

Many people have asked me if I would consider mixing and selling that mix. Steve himself urged me to do it. But no—that's not for me! If I can't even quite get it together for my own garden on a regular basis, I'm not the one to make it for others. I'm sure there's a good business model in there for someone, though. It would be very simple to just buy a few sacks of the mix each gardening season, but hunting down all the bits and pieces isn't fun.

Not when we can just go pick up cow manure or make some simple compost piles.

So back to compost. Compost is the reason I originally jumped into this digression on Steve's Mix. If we want nutrient density in my food, we should start with a nutrient-dense way to feed the garden.

Our compost pile can be that. Into it, we can put ashes, eggshells, spoiled seafood, coffee grounds, offal, fish wastes, wood ashes, tree leaves, all sorts of kitchen scraps, seaweed, rotten fruit and plenty more. Each of these ingredients adds a different area of nutrients to the mix. A good, critter-proof compost pile can compost plenty more than you think. Stop following those lists of what you "can" and "can't" compost and start composting everything organic. The nutrient-density of, say, chicken livers is WAY BETTER than the nutrient-density of wilted lettuce. So throw them in.

Noah Sanders, author of *Born-Again Dirt*, shared with me the discovery that lime added to a compost pile was significantly more effective at providing calcium to plants than lime dusted on the garden. Once passed through the magic of the compost pile and bound up into humus loaded with lots of microlife, amendments apparently become much more available to plants.

As much of what most Americans eat is coming from all over the map and is grown or raised on a variety of soils with different nutrient profiles, chances are you are getting a good bit of variation in micronutrients from your compost pile, and those micros end up in your garden when you apply that finished compost.

Instead of saving bananas for potassium and eggshells for calcium and bones for phosphorus and manure for nitrogen and all that, why not just throw everything into one big pile and let nature sort it out? I read a book that talked about how to make specialized fertilizers for all kinds of special applications. It reminded me of when I was a kid and I would pretend I had a laboratory and would make all sorts of experimental compounds that I would bottle in old baby food jars. One concoction was made by adding some yeast to flour and water and letting it bubble away until it stopped, then I would let it dry out in the carport where it would get infested with insects. The final, blackened remains I would then mix with water to make a black solution I called Compound X.

It was very powerful for something, I'm sure. Probably treated spider mites. Or cured cancer. Anyhow, the desire is there to sort and dry and sift and mix and label and create various magical potions for our gardens; yet plants don't really need all that. They are very good at taking what they need from what they can find. Like when we caught a rat in a trap, then buried the rat and the trap in a hole and mounded soil over the top, then planted a few pumpkin seeds on top.

Those vines did great and produced plenty of fruit! Much better than my rat-free pumpkins growing a little ways away. We didn't measure how much calcium was in that rat. Or how much nitrogen. Or molybdenum. We just buried a nice, nutrient-dense rat and the plant roots took what they wanted.

If you give your plants cow manure, they'll get plenty of humus and lots of minerals from all the grass and greenery the cow consumed. If you give your plants compost, they'll get a wide range of minerals from whatever went into the compost.

Instead of trying to mix everything perfectly as I tried with my Steve's Mix experiment, I now just think about what might be missing and try to throw a little of that into the compost that will end up on the garden beds. Realistically, though, if you're eating some produce and meat from off-farm and you add it to your compost pile or swamp water, you're probably getting at least some of what you need. If you're worried, just throw in some ocean seaweed or buy a little kelp meal to fill out the micros. I still do that on occasion.

Over the last few years I have realized that my fertilizing was getting too complicated. The balancing of ratios and numbers isn't a bad thing and some people love it, but it was an unnecessary complexity in my gardening. Never having the "right" food for my plants brought me a vague feeling of obligation and guilt as I gardened. There was always this reminder of "Oh, wait, I need to make some more fertilizer mix!" and I don't need that anymore. Talking to Noah was freeing. I'll just go back to what I always did and throw everything in the compost, then use that to keep the gardens happy. With abundant cow manure to add as well, my life is easy. As the winter comes upon us, we also generate lots of wood ash for raising the soil pH and giving us the final piece we need.

Yet here is something to remember: though we talk about "feeding our plants," the reality is that we need to add nutrients to the soil so the plants can take what they want. It's not really feeding plants—it's feeding nutrients into the soil.

As Robert Pavlis writes in *Soil Science for Gardeners:*

> Most gardeners fertilize because someone said they should do it, or some online source suggested it. They do it in the mistaken belief that plants need to be fed; this is completely wrong. You do not fertilize plants. You fertilize to replace missing nutrients in soil.... The idea we must feed the plant seems to make perfect sense, but it ignores a critical point. They get their food from the soil solution. You don't add fertilizer to plants—you add it to soil.... Plants absorb the nutrients they need from the soil. If grass needs more nitrogen, it takes more nitrogen from the soil than a plant that needs less. If a plant is ready to bloom and it needs more phosphorus, it takes more from the soil. Your job is to keep nutrient levels high enough so that plants never run short.

Feed the soil and the soil will feed you.

One of the marvelous things about feeding with compost is that the nutrients are all in there, slowly breaking down into the soil. Plants can pull whatever they want from that reserve. Lasagna gardening and deep mulch methods keep plants happier for much longer than if you just till up an area and throw down some 10-10-10. Most chemical fertilizers wash through the soil quickly, giving plants a quick hit before disappearing. Compost is a steady, slow-release nutrient source. Learn how to make and use it. Unless you really want to be totally minimalist and just use that wood ash with some urine...

No. We're minimalist enough. Let's move on.

Chapter 5

Watering Made Easy

The easiest way to garden is to garden with the rain. Some climates lend themselves to this and some don't. We are halfway between, as we get abundant rainfall interspersed with weeks or even months of drought.

Yet we can still grow most crops on just the rainfall provided we have enough organic matter in the soil and we space out our plants. I learned this method from—yet again—Steve Solomon. If you have more space and plant your crops far apart, they can often go without irrigation.

As he writes in *Water-Wise Gardening*:

> Before the mid-1970s, American garden books said to arrange most vegetables in long single rows with footpaths between each row. Between-row spacing for most vegetables usually ranged from three to four feet. The distance between rows had as much to do with the amount of anticipated summertime rainfall as it did with the type of vegetable. Sprawling crops like winter squash, cucumber and most tomato varieties were allowed even more space between rows. Small-sized vegetables like carrot and beet

might be assigned a pair of parallel rows with a foot between them, the center of each pair of rows three or four feet to the next row with a footpath between them. In the eastern half of the United States and Canada all but a few kinds of vegetables can successfully forage for moisture when grown that way. In 1979 when I went into the vegetable garden seed business the average backyard food garden was 1,000 square feet. I think the average house lot prior to the mid-1970s was about 15,000 square feet, 3/8 acre. In small towns it was ½ acre.

Summertime rainfall usually comes often enough and in large enough quantity to be sufficient for vegetable gardening in any part of the United States where the native vegetation had been forest. The main use for irrigation was to help germinate seeds; it was done using hose and nozzle or a watering can. Once seedlings were up and growing, rainfall took care of it. When there was an unusually dry summer the vegetable garden might be watered a few times, usually with lawn sprinklers. Garden books of that era paid little or no attention to irrigation.

In the mid 1970s a new method called "intensive" was introduced by a West Coast guru named John Jeavons. His book How To Grow More Vegetables Than You Ever Thought Possible On Less Land Than You Ever Imagined has been through innumerable revisions and is still in print. Jeavons' basic idea is that by using wide super-fertile raised beds and decreasing interplant spacing as much as possible, yield from a given space could be greatly increased. My own experience with this system says this assertion is as much hyperbole as it is truth.

Jeavons' method was strongly promoted and soon was broadly accepted. By the mid-1980s every vegetable gardening book writer (except myself), every magazine article and every extension service publication intended for gardeners was regurgitating Jeavons' methods. I think the underlying conditions favoring Jeavons' narrative were population pressure, inflation and with it a steady erosion of real prosperity that was forcing new homes to be built on ever-smaller lots. I think it highly likely that The Powers That Be wanted the ever-harder-struggling average person to believe that a postage stamp garden could be as productive as a much larger one.

One thing about intensive food gardening is absolutely certain: the method requires frequent irrigation because densely planted beds can be sucked dry after a few hot sunny summer days. This might be okay as long as there is plenty of irrigation water available. It also makes the garden as needy of care as a pet can be when the family goes on holiday.

If you'd like to avoid setting up an irrigation system, just remember: wider spacing = less watering.

We've also found that deep mulch/lasagna garden beds require much less irrigation, especially after they start to rot down a bit. That thick layer of mulch makes a big difference.

You may see a big, widely spaced garden as a bunch of wasted space, yet remember: it's not a waste when you consider the time and water that goes into regularly irrigating a smaller space.

Another thing to consider: mulch slows the impact of rainfall while also increasing the infiltration of water. Cover crops do the same. If rain hits hard, dry ground, it tends to run away with it, washing soil towards the lowest point of your property, or off it altogether. If you have living soil, covered with plants and filled with roots and fungi, the rain flows down into the soil rather than running off the surface.

Iowa State University notes:

> The most effective way to control erosion is to maintain a permanent surface cover on the soil surface, such as pasture or meadow. Therefore, areas that are highly susceptible to water or wind erosion need to be considered for soil conservation programs. Soil losses in Iowa due to water erosion and surface runoff can contribute a great deal to surface water quality concerns.
>
> Many studies indicate that soil erosion results in large decreases in soil productivity. In a study conducted at Iowa State University on 40 soil associations, Craft and coworkers (*Proceedings of the National Symposium on Erosion and Soil Productivity*, 1984) reported that the impact of soil erosion on soil productivity was largely determined by subsoil properties because they effect root growth, soil water availability, and plow layer fertility. Thus, the loss of the topsoil can have considerable impact on yield, where nutrient availability, root growth environment, and soil water availability are essential for plant development. In soils with unfavorable subsoil conditions, erosion can have

WATERING MADE EASY

a large effect on productivity, if the plow layer soil fertility is not restored.

Plant residue management is another way of controlling soil erosion by intercepting raindrops, thereby reducing surface runoff and protecting soil surface particle detachment by raindrop impact. Crop residue can provide an excellent soil cover after harvest and enhance snow harvesting during the off season, improve soil water intake by preventing soil surface sealing due to raindrop impact, and consequently, reduce surface runoff. Equally important in minimizing soil erosion is the adoption of a cropping system along with conservation tillage practices such as no-till, strip-till, and ridge-till. The degree of effectiveness of different tillage practices depends on the degree of soil manipulation, which effects the residue distribution on the soil surface.[6]

In general, the less bare ground you leave, the better.

If you really need to get food fast and lack mulch, do what you can. You can go ahead and till, then grow single-row gardens. It works. But over time, you should be thinking about how to keep and build the soil you have via cover-cropping and/or mulching. We've been experimenting with growing plants as mulch and compost materials. In our area, Sudan-sorghum grass and sunn hemp both grow rapidly and produce a lot of biomass we can use to cover the ground. In our food forest and Grocery Row Gardens, we also grow *Tithonia diversifolia* and various canna species as chop-and-drop plants to keep the ground covered. Tree prunings, dead weeds, fall leaves, grass clippings... all can go into your gardens.

Sometimes, however, mulch can be an issue with annual gardens. The reason I don't recommend mulch for every single garden is two-fold. First, it can be really hard to gather enough materials to mulch a large family garden, so sometimes we need to just press on and grow food without it. Second, in some climates mulch can harbor a lot of insect life that loves to eat tender annuals. One friend with a deep-mulched garden told me she can't start anything from seed because the bugs will eat it when it's tiny. If you have this problem, you might want to grow transplants to put out when they're big enough to survive a hungry cutworm or two, or wait on the mulch until your seedlings are bigger. Or just annual garden without mulch and save your mulch for your tougher perennial crops. It's hard to create a one-size-fits-all recommendation, so even though I believe that mulch is usually beneficial, it may not *always* be beneficial.

Simple Irrigation

I must confess: my favorite way to irrigate is to water with the garden hose. I like to spend time in the garden, so when we have a dry spell I really don't mind going out with the hose and spending some time soaking everything.

However, we don't always have time for that, so the backup plan is to use a simple tripod-mounted sprinkler we got from the local hardware store. It's simple, and we can put it as far as the hose stretches, then move it around as need be.

In my old North Florida garden my friend Allan helped me put in some PVC pipes beneath the garden and we put stand pipes up from that about 5' in the air and attached sprinkler heads to them. All we had to do then was to turn a handle and it would rain on the garden from three sprinklers, covering the entire growing area. This was great, since we had a well. City water is more expensive, and may have more chlorine and/or chloramines in it than you might like. Not to mention other chemicals that may or may not turn the frogs gay.

Our gardens always look the best after a rain, however, so we try to focus on making the best use of rainwater by keeping the ground covered with mulch and plants so the water soaks in and erosion doesn't take place. Keeping the water that falls is better than having it run off, and then dragging the sprinkler out a couple days after a rain to water yet again.

Drip Irrigation

For years I have read Mark and Anna at *The Walden Effect*[7]. My thoughts are the same as theirs on the disadvantages of drip irrigation. As they write:

> Most high tech farmers will tell you that drip irrigation is the best possible method to water your garden. In some ways they are right — drip irrigation minimizes your water usage by putting the water just where your plants need it.

You don't lose water to evaporation and you don't waste water by irrigating your aisles along with your garden beds. I have seen professional organic farmers use drip irrigation very effectively, stringing long pipes under black plastic in raised rows.

However, for our purposes, drip irrigation failed us. Here's why:

- Drip irrigation depends on extremely clean water. The tiniest particle of mud sucked up by our creek pump quickly clogged the holes in our irrigation system, which meant that the soil around the clogged holes got no water. If you plan to install drip irrigation with anything except city water, you will need to install a serious filter and change it regularly.
- Drip irrigation requires a lot of hoses and they have to be moved every year if you practice crop rotation. Drip hoses with holes two feet apart for watering tomatoes will do that bed no good once you replace the tomatoes with onions spaced three inches apart.
- Drip irrigation is made for row crops, not for beds. I like to maximize space in my permanent raised beds by planting some crops — carrots, lettuce, greens, etc. — scattered across the entire surface. Drip irrigation just doesn't work for this setup.
- Drip irrigation is expensive. I'm a skinflint. Enough said.
- To maximize the longevity of those expensive drip hoses, you need to put them under a mulch to prevent UV damage to the plastic. Since most farmers don't have enough organic mulch to cover their entire garden, they usually end

> up covering the rows with that awful black plastic. Evil, evil, evil!
>
> All of that said, we do use drip irrigation for our perennial bush fruit. There, we made the drip hoses ourselves out of 1 inch pipe that a friend was throwing out, drilling holes much larger than those found in storebought drip hoses. In permanent plantings, drip irrigation does work wonders.[8]

The on-the-ground experience we've had is the same as that of Mark and Anna. It's a pain to set up, looks ugly, needs tweaking and fiddling, plus squirrels chew holes in the system to get the water.

Stand pipes are simpler all around.

Watering Cans

If you want to get even more simple—and you have a small garden—you can simply get a few watering cans and carry them to your plants. We have a rain barrel on our porch we dip watering cans into, then carry them to various locations. It works well on a small scale, but when you have a lot to water, watering cans aren't the best.

Fertigation

Fertigation is one of the most powerful ways to jumpstart plant growth. "Fertigation" comes from merging two words:

fertilizing and irrigation. It just means that there is some fertilizer in the water you use for irrigation. Since plant roots do quite well absorbing nutrients from water flowing through the soil, this method feeds the garden excellently. It also gives them much more tolerance to drought, when compared to simply watering with water alone.

If you've ever mixed some Peter's Plant Food crystals into water and used it to feed some unhappy ivy, you've fertigated. Or if you've dumped a cup of coffee into a potted *Dracaena*.

My friend Elizabeth has a clever system that siphons fluid from a couple of liquid fertilizer barrels and mixes it into the well water she sprays from a sprinkler about 8' up above her garden beds. In one barrel she had mostly rotting fish guts in water, and in the other she has swamp water made from various weeds and herbs. She can switch between the barrels or pull from both of them by turning a handle or two.

This is a little bit above our engineering pay grade, but it does make for very happy gardens.

We used to keep some old hot tubs as ponds in our gardens, and would irrigate from them, knowing there was some aquatic plants, muck, fish manure and insect larvae in the water. All good fertigation ingredients!

I also saw a great system Geoff Lawton designed where there was a duck pond uphill, with a large PVC pipe running from it down to the gardens below. When you turned on the tap, a torrent of green-brown duck manure water shot out of the pipe. That stuff is garden gold!

Keep your watering systems simple, and if there's a way to add a little fertilizer to the water supply, go for it.

Chapter 6

You Can Do Everything with a Machete

Down in the Caribbean we witnessed machetes being used for a much wider range of tasks than you might think. Keepers of bulls, goats and sheep always carried machetes, and in the woods you'd see them slashing down fast-growing jungle trees and brush for their animals every morning.

Machetes were also used to dig holes. Before one public holiday as a park was being spiffied up, we witnessed government employees digging tree planting holes with machetes. Machetes were also used as a trowel for transplanting vegetables.

You could also use your machete to harvest fruit, and then to peel the fruit you harvested.

Machetes were used to harvest cinnamon bark as well. Limbs were chopped down, then the outer bark was scraped away and the inner bark slit and peeled from the branch to be dried.

Machetes were used for catching land crabs to sell at market or to cook for household use. A man would find a crab burrow, then stick his machete through the soil a couple feet behind the entrance, keeping a crab from retreating. He would then reach into the dark burrow and yank out the crab, paying little attention to the pinches received in the process.

When the electric company sent men out to clean up the power lines, they would often a worker up a ladder into the trees with (you guessed it) a machete. He'd slash and prune his way around the wires as a couple of men yelled instructions at him from the ground.

Machetes were even used in home furniture making. Woodworkers who made rough-hewn chairs and tables and other useful objects were often called "cutlass carpenters" for their extensive machete use.

We assisted in more than one neighborhood butchering day where a bull was dispatched by slitting his throat with a machete. After death, the animal was laid on top of a spread of banana leaves to be skinned and gutted with kitchen knives—and machetes. When the fine work was done, a machete was used to hack the bones and meat into pieces to be sold at the roadside. Every time you had a stew, you had to watch for all the bone shards. Even the main butcher shop in town had an array of tables manned by men and women with machetes, chopping and weighing out hunks of bright red flesh as the tropical sun streamed in the windows and the chatter of shoppers filled the air. The fish market was very similar. Razor-sharp machetes were used to gut and slice huge fresh tuna and snapper into manageable sizes.

It's remarkable how many uses you can get from a single tool. The machete is so versatile that I almost titled this book *Machete Gardening*. In our gardens we use machetes for chopping and dropping cover crops and nutrient accumulating perennials, as well as for transplanting, chopping materials for the compost pile, stirring fertilizer solutions, digging transplant holes, clearing pathways, dispatching poisonous snakes, digging up roots, harvesting sugarcane and cassava, taking cuttings, butchering chickens, stirring coals, peeling fruit, slicing up potatoes and yams for planting, and even smacking flies and hornets.

You can do a lot with a machete. Sometimes we feel like we need to get a whole bunch of different tools, yet we can often "stack functions" by using certain tools for multiple tasks. There really aren't a lot of tools you "need" for your garden. Almost everything can be done with a machete. Mike and I cleared acres of grass and weeds with just machetes.

Start with the simple things: a spade, a fork, perhaps a broadfork and a grub hoe, and a machete. You need a machete.

I've explained all the other tools before, so there's no need to run over them.

Just grab your machete first—you might be surprised how many things you can accomplish with just one tool.

Chapter 7

Grow the Simple Stuff

I went to my fridge and started pulling out jars of seeds. Each jar was large and contained a variety of seed packets pressed together inside. Beads of sweat crowded together on my forehead. My hands trembled as I set the jars on the table. Some of the jars were labeled with words like "summer," or "corn," or "greens," others lacked labels and contained unsorted packets jumbled together in sheaves.

I opened the "corn" jar and pulled out multiple packets of heirloom grain corn varieties. Some were blue, some red, others gold, blue, white, speckled or multicolored. On the packets were quaint origin stories about the varieties.

I took a deep breath and ripped open one packet, then another, then another, dumping the grains together on the table like a trove of gems, mixing up the effort of generations. One variety came from an Iowa farmer in the 40s... another from a seed company in the 1800s... yet another from a backyard breeder in Vermont... some were from a Thanksgiving Indian corn display... and a handful came from my friends Danny and Wanda at Deep South Homestead in Mississippi.

Now they were all together in one pile. And once I had that pile, I scooped it off the table into a single jar and went outside to plant the kernels in my garden. Down the rows I went, dropping a pink kernel... then a yellow... then a green, a brown, a white, a blue... all together in seven glorious rows in a single big bed of grain corn!

For years I had carefully saved varieties, trying to grow enough individuals of each type to maintain varieties. In one patch I'd grow Hickory King, in another I'd try out Oaxacan Green Dent corn. Sometimes I even planted corn across multiple properties. One year I had corn in two separate patches on my own land plus another variety on a relative's property. Keeping varieties from crossing while still maintaining enough individual plants to avoid inbreeding depression was hard work.

This year I was done.

I covered over my newly planted rows and watered them in. I decided not to baby the patch. I would let the rain take care of them, and just feed a few times with swamp water. A week after planting, sprouts began to emerge. As they grew I could see a big difference in the plants. Some had red stems, some were green, some were purple. Some stalks were squat, others lean and tall. Some grew very fast and others didn't.

I looked forward to seeing what would happen when they started setting ears.

The summer was brutal, going from flooding rain to extreme drought and then back to flooding rain. My corn patch struggled, but about half of the plants managed to set ears. The ears were mostly small and some were stolen by squirrels. Others rotted in the rain. Over time, I still got some that dried down enough for me to harvest. As I did, I found very entertaining mixes of kernels. Some ears were mostly one color with a scattering of different-colored kernels in the rows; others were completely mixed up. If you do this, you can create robust varieties that are bred to survive in your climate, with your own growing methods.

Now where did we get this crazy idea? I'll get to that in a minute.

I had been interested in breeding new varieties for some years, thanks to the work of Carol Deppe, author of *Breed Your Own Vegetable Varieties*. I took what I learned from her and started crossing pumpkin varieties, working towards creating a large-fruited and super vigorous Seminole pumpkin variety. Our multiple moves took a toll on that project, however, and we ended up losing the seed lines. Later I mixed up multiple Maxima pumpkins and had good results, but the awful weather of early 2022 almost ended that line as well. In 2021 we harvested over 400lbs of various pumpkins; in 2022, we didn't get a single one. It was like a curse hung over the sandpit we were renting, and despite all my tricks, I lost all I'd planted to first frost, then drought, then small chewing insects, then to flooding rain, then to vine borers and burrowing animals, then burning heat and drought again. It was a ridiculously bad year for weather and we had ridiculously bad soil that was tough to overcome even in a good year. It happens!

Sometimes God allows us to experience failure and tough times so we appreciate our blessings more. If you've ever been sick for a week and then recovered, it's like getting a new life again.

Every year's garden is a chance to start again. We pick up the tattered remnants of our previous year's seeds and cuttings and carry them through to the next, where they get a chance to grow again and hopefully do much better. Especially if we are able to let nature select out the genetics that thrive in our backyard. At least, that's what Joseph Lofthouse argues in his book *Landrace Gardening*. He was the one who originally gave us complete permission to break down the genetic walls between our heirloom seed lines. When I wrote my book *Compost Everything*, it was based on years of throwing out complicated lists of dos and don'ts and getting composting back down to its essentials. Lofthouse is doing the same for seed-saving and plant breeding. In reading his book I discovered a kindred spirit. Despite very different backgrounds, experiences, and location, we had both realized that our respective areas of study had become cluttered with lots of unnecessary baggage. I tossed out the inviolable and sacred rules of composting whereas he took a wrecking ball to the precious world of heirloom seed saving. Lofthouse's manifesto on creating your own local landrace varieties immediately resonated with me.

In short, he urges his readers to mix together a wide range

of varieties and then to half-neglect the garden in order to bring forward the most vigorous plants. Replant what lives and perhaps add a few more varieties. The first step, then, becomes breeding a variety for survival in your garden and climate. Then, after that, you can start selecting for other traits you want, such as color, taste, shape, size, rapidity of production, etc.

Thanks to him, this year I've decided to take many of the vegetable varieties in my fridge and mix them together. I've got a seed collection worthy of any hoarder. There are perhaps a dozen radish varieties in the fridge, and a half-dozen types of cabbage. Plenty of pole beans and bush beans, lots of tomatoes, lots of lettuces, and lots of pumpkins and squash. Why not quit worrying about types and trying to keep them sorted?

I can just take all my bush beans out of their various packets and put them in one jar labeled "bush beans." I can do the same with the pole beans. And I can cross up all the radishes and lettuces. Why not?

A quick note here on plant breeding. Not all vegetables cross readily. Beans, for instance, rarely cross since they naturally self-pollinate. Tomatoes do the same. Pumpkins inside a species will cross readily, but are less likely to hybridize with other species of pumpkin. This means your Tan Cheese pumpkin and your butternut squash—both *Curcurbita moschata* cultivars—will give you entertaining crosses, but that butternut is much less likely to cross with your Blue

Hubbards, which are a *C. Maxima* variety. I'm no Luther Burbank, that's for sure, but if I can get to just one percent of his talent, I'll be light years ahead of the curve. Earlier this year I scored the entire 1914 illustrated 12-volume hardcover set of *Luther Burbank: His Methods and Discoveries* on ebay and plan to read through it over the next year to see what I can learn and apply. (My mom once told me I was an elitist, and perhaps I am. I'm certainly a book snob, which is probably a character failing, yet here I am bragging about it. It's a hopeless case. Just yesterday I left a five-volume edition of St. Thomas Aquinas' *Summa Theologica* on my wife's side of the bed and told her I had bought her some "light summer reading.")

I don't expect my beans to cross much, but mixing them together does minimize our messy seed hoard. And it's going to be fun to see yellow wax and purple Romas growing side-by-side in the rows, and the baskets of lovely bean mixes will look great in the kitchen. We'll also be able to save seeds from the plants that do the best, over time establishing the types that thrive best in our garden. The turnips and radishes and pumpkins will be another story. In the first year they'll all look just like they did on the packages—then the fun begins, as the second generation gives us interesting crosses unlike anything else. Old commercial varieties and hybrids and carefully saved heirlooms will join together over time into Good Gardens specials that are better adapted to our garden. Most seed varieties were selected and inbred to give consistent results in specific locations. We're taking all those far-flung genes and letting them re-sort and select into types that fit how we plant and feed and cultivate in our climate. Then we can select traits we find interesting and grow our own heirlooms.

This spring we planted a bunch of different pickling cucumber varieties together along with seeds we crossed and saved last year. We got almost 200lbs of cucumbers in the spring, plus we now have jars worth of crossed-up seeds. One of my sons has also been crossing watermelon varieties together for multiple years, and this year we have some very vigorous vines in the garden which keep sending beautiful watermelons into the kitchen. Some look like Charleston Gray, some like Sugar Baby, some like Congo, some like crosses—and they just keep coming and coming. We've had red, orange, yellow and pink melons so far, with different shapes, sizes and flavors. It's way more fun than just planting one type, as we're hunting for interesting genetic combinations while also adapting watermelons to our Lower Alabama backyard.

One of the melons that came in was a rich red color inside and had the most wonderful flavor we've ever encountered. It almost tasted like lychee fruit, with an interesting hint of rose petals. Those seeds got saved alone, and we'll see if we can stabilize that line separately from the others.

As we did with composting, simplifying down to "throw it on the ground," we will now do with seeds. Just "plant them in the ground" and let them run together into a wide mix of genetics that will give us fun crosses and interesting results.

Who knows? We may even get to name our own varieties of vegetables in a few years.

For years I've recommended planting a bunch of different cultivars of plants and seeing what works best in your garden. *Totally Crazy Easy Florida Gardening* was based on the experiments we did with planting crops from across the earth and then replanting and building a base set of reliable food-producers from the ones that did well. We had great results with that method. This is just a deeper application of the same method. Instead of just selecting, we now cultivate what may turn out to be even better varieties that didn't exist before. What a great experiment—and what a great way to minimize your seed collection.

Gardening With Perennials

Most of us start our gardening careers with annuals. The first food plant I ever grew was green beans. What I discovered over time, however, was that perennials that fit my climate were even easier to grow and maintain than annuals. My old cucumbers and radishes are long-gone, but the trees I planted in my parents' yard and on later homesteads of my own continue to grow, sometimes decades after I put them in the ground. If you wish to eliminate a lot of work in your gardening and don't have the time to carefully tend annuals, why not plant trees every year? They complain less, and often live even when neglected. A patch of beans is gone in a few months, and if you don't water, weed and feed it well, it could be gone faster than that. But a well-established tree takes a bit of work at the beginning and then keeps going. A few years later, it starts fruiting, and then has the capability—deer, disease, flood and drought permitting—to make bushels of fruit for the rest of your life and beyond. Two years ago we harvested at least a hundred pounds of pears from two gigantic pear trees planted back in the 70s by a neighbor. Though the neighbors were not great gardeners and didn't maintain much of anything other than their grass, that bit of forward thinking is still paying dividends.

In his excellent book *Tree Crops*, J. Russell Smith observes the ruined landscapes and erosion and destruction caused by annual-based agriculture—corn in particular—and argues that we should redirect our focus to long-term tree-based production of food. Before King Corn took over large swaths of America, there were forests filled with various nut trees, including chestnuts, hickories, acorns, walnuts, pecans and more. The chestnut was almost eradicated by the arrival of blight from the far east, but many other nut trees remained. Smith argued that if we used even a fraction of our corn-breeding resources to instead develop and breed tree crops, America could feed herself on the bounty of the forests. Large low-tannin acorns could be selected and bred, blight-resistant chestnuts could be encouraged and planted, honey locust could be improved in yield and used as carb-rich cattle fodder—the possibilities are incredible.

Yet, for the most part, Smith's vision was discarded in favor of more and more annual agriculture. It seems that most people are not capable of thinking long term or are simply too lazy to put in multi-generational work.

It's intoxicating how fast annual crops grow. In fact, that is their main attraction. You can get a radish in 30 days, beans in 50, pumpkins in 100. The fastest-yielding fruit "tree" I know of is papaya, which takes about a year to bear fruit... from seed! After that, from seed, peaches usually bear in 3 years or so, apples can take 6–8, avocados may take 6–10, pecans will take a decade... it's a long, long wait for a hungry gardener.

Some of this wait time can be cut down by grafting, of course. You don't have to wait eight years for a mango to bear if you simply start a seedling, let it grow for six months, then graft scion wood from a fruiting tree onto it. That will shorten your wait to 2–3 years. Yet in that time period, you could have grown multiple crops of nice, fat watermelons—which only take around 90–100 days to produce!

You see the attraction, don't you? When I was a kid and went looking for seeds to plant in my garden, I would often pick packets that had very short yield times. I loved beans and radishes. Waiting more than a month or two for a plant to produce seemed like forever to my eight-year-old self.

Now that I am decades older, waiting longer is not a chore. I think in years, rather than days. When we buy a new homestead, we always plant some short crops like potatoes, turnips and cassava—but at the same time, we also plant fruit trees, some of which will take years to bear. Many of them were started from seed. They'll take their time, sure, but bit by bit, they'll start producing and unlike corn or peas or radishes, they'll produce year after year after year. Many of these trees will outlive me and keep producing for future generations.

Case closed, right? Perennial plants win. Plant forests and stop tilling!

Not quite. As much value as there is in orchards, woodlands and food forest projects, it also makes sense to practice annual gardening. A decade ago, I almost convinced myself that food forests were the end-all form of gardening and gave up my vegetable beds... yet I didn't. I couldn't. We needed the food!

The marvelous thing about annual gardens is how much food they can produce. It is really hard to replace the yield of melons, potatoes, turnips, pumpkins and other annual crops with a tree-based system. Eventually, it may be possible—and the overall yield of biomass, fruit, cooking wood, etc. in a forest will be higher—yet the straight-up food yield and quick turnover of annual gardens is unbeatable.

Think of your annual garden as a sprint and your orchard as a long march. There are times for both. It makes sense to balance a homestead about 50-50 between annuals and perennials. You can get your starchy tubers and grains and greens and hot peppers and tomatoes from the ground and your nuts and fruits from the trees. Every year when we plant annual gardens, we also plant trees and bushes that may bear years later. At the beginning of establishing a homestead, you'll have lots more coming from your annual gardens whereas your orchard/food forest/edible hedges, etc., will be bearing little to no yield. A few years later, your annual gardens will still be producing a lot but the perennial crops will be catching up. Though they may never outyield your annual gardens—provided you work the soil diligently—the trees will eventually bear you a large amount of yield with much less work. As you get older, this is a very good thing. When my grandparents were older, they didn't grow vegetable gardens, but they sure picked a lot of fruit from the tangerine, key lime and mango trees that had been started decades before.

The lure of annuals is a quick yield. The lure of perennials is the long-term ease of production.

Both have their place. You may lean more towards one or the other. As for me, I'm now balanced in the middle. You can grow annuals without wrecking the environment and causing the destruction Smith witnessed. Heck, a heavily sprayed and fertilized orchard can also cause damage to the environment. As is often the case, balance is key. Plant a lot of different trees and plants and manage them without resorting to poisons. Over time, some will thrive and some will not. Discard the failures and reinforce the successes. There's a place for perennials and a place for annuals.

I've combined them both in my Grocery Row Gardening system, where we make nice mounded beds, then plant them with a mix of fruit trees, annual and perennial vegetables, berries, medicinal herbs, pollinator plants, various root crops and nitrogen-fixers.

To make a Grocery Row Garden bed, till up a big area and grab some stakes (we use short pieces of rebar) and hammer in two of them at one end of the new bed, 4' apart. Now pull twine down to where you want to put in the other side of the bed and do the same thing. The strings should be exactly parallel at 4' in width for the entire length of the bed. If the entire area is well-tilled, it should then be easy to shovel out loose soil from the space on either side of the bed—which will soon be pathways—into the bed, giving you a nice, rounded mound of loose soil, 4' wide by however long you choose. Most of my beds are about 80' in length right now. If you have a smaller yard, however, it's no big deal to make 8' beds, or 10' or 20'.

Once you've made your first bed, mark off your second 4' wide bed 3' away and repeat the process until you've made all the beds you're ready to make. Starting with at least three beds makes sense, as it's a nice, balanced-looking garden with lots of good "edge" space for maximum yields.

Now it's time to plant your fruit trees. We plant them 12' apart. This would be rather tight spacing if you were to simply let them grow to full size, but you're not going to do that! As they get bigger, your job is to prune them back so they never get taller than about 8' in height. This will allow you to grow vegetables beneath them without completely shading them out. Once you have your trees planted at 12' intervals in your first bed, it's time to plant the second bed. In that second bed, plant the trees at an alternate diagonal spacing to the first bed, giving them more breathing room than being spaced 7' across from each other on opposite sides of the path. It's like a zig-zag when viewed from above. Alternately, you can simply skip the trees in alternate beds and plant shrubs or vines instead, like rabbiteye blueberries or grapes on trellises. We sometimes put shorter shrubs in the in-between beds, alternating a bed planted with fruit trees with a bed planted with shrubs. That way if the pruning was neglected in the future we'd still have tons of space.

Once the trees are in, plant more perennials around their bases, or fill up all the remaining space with annual crops. We grow a lot of potatoes, sweet potatoes, radishes, brassicas, hot peppers and tomatoes in our Grocery Row Gardens. As we feed and water these short crops, the trees also get care and grow faster than the trees we plant be themselves out in the yard.

If you find that we just don't have time to take care of an annual garden, no worries! Just don't plant annuals and keep the ground mulched or mowed to prevent weeds from taking over. Now your Grocery Row Garden is an orchard. Those perennials will just keep going.

It's just another option for gardeners who want to simplify. You don't have to slave away in the garden forever and ever. Some years are just bad years for annuals and sometimes we don't have time to bother with them. If you have lots of fruit and nut trees and shrubs growing, you'll still have good food from your homestead even in those crazy years.

Plant long-term as you plant short-term and you'll reap the rewards for decades to come.

Chapter 8

Grapes on Trees and Other Stories

When we lived on the Caribbean island of Grenada, we discovered how much we didn't need. We had a composting toilet system, a couple of tiny cabins, an outdoor shower made from reclaimed roofing panels framed out around a large volcanic boulder, and a large garden we worked with only hand tools. Anything more complicated was quite expensive, as those of you living on islands will understand. Trying to get a tiller or a woodchipper was difficult, and if you could find one, it was exorbitantly expensive. When I wanted to do some landscape painting, I was unable to find an easel for sale and canvases were of poor quality and cost way too much.

So we made do. I made an easel from a few straight tree limbs bolted together, and made a paint carrier from a short piece of rope and an old coffee can. We also got boards from a sawmill to paint on instead of using canvas, and primed them with gesso. The brushes and paints we imported in our luggage, but that was it.

As we worked in our tropical garden, people watching over YouTube would often say things like "why don't you use a chainsaw?" or "you should get wood chips," but both of those things were very hard to come by. So we used what we had. And yet, we had one of the best gardens we'd ever made. Piece by piece we reclaimed ground from the jungle with machetes and shovels, a bow saw, a fork and some cow manure and ashes for fertilizer, along with homemade compost and lots of chopped-and-dropped tropical grasses and greenery. We watched and learned from the local farmers and saw how they got great yields with just hard work and simple tools.

Throughout history there have been simple solutions to agricultural needs. In this chapter, we'll cover some shortcuts to modern methods that require purchased goods and power tools. You really can do a lot with very little.

Like growing grapes, for example.

Grapes on Trees

Something that strikes me repeatedly as I practice gardening is how many ways there are to grow food and cultivate plants. As soon as you think you've found "the right method," you find another one that seems better. At our last property we built a small vineyard with power poles and wire. It's the "proper" single-row system often used in Florida muscadine production.

But it's by no means the only method. It may not even be the best method, even though it's common and easy to construct. There are many methods that can be used. Like growing grape vines on trees!

Reader Andrew Wallace emailed me a fascinating article covering the "married vine" method of growing grapes, as practiced in ancient Italy and recorded on the website of the Guado al Melo vineyard in Italy:

> The Etruscans were the first winegrowers in Italy, beginning from the wild varieties.
>
> The wild grapevine is a local plant in the Mediterranean area. In the more ancient times, people began to gather its fruits in the woods....
>
> The Etruscans cultivated vines in the same manner they saw these plants grow wild in the woods. The vine is a climbing shrub, a species of liana. In a wood, its natural environment in our latitudes, it tends to climb up a tree to reach the light as possible (it is very heliophilous species). However, it is not a parasite: the vine does not weaken the tree on which it clings.
>
> Today the Etruscan cultivation system name is "married vine", *"vite maritata"* in Italian. It's as if the vine is "married" to the tree.[9]

We have not incorporated grapevines into our food forest systems yet, as they are often too vigorous for young trees, and we keep moving before the system gets big enough to handle them. However, our current property has a wide variety of trees of various sizes which we can use for viticulture experiments. In fact, there is a row of popcorn trees along the driveway. Wouldn't it be interesting if they worked? Their allelopathic tendencies might be bad for grapes, but who knows? We planted some vines beside a few of them this spring just to see.

We also have a young pecan tree, some black cherries, some sweet gums and even a black walnut that might work as supports for grape vines.

In an article titled "The historical relationship of elms and vines", by P. Fuentes-Utrilla, R. A. López-Rodríguez, and L. Gil at the Universidad Politécnica de Madrid, we read:

> Many Roman books on Agriculture have lasted to the present day. Cato's *De Agri Cultura* (2nd Century BC) is the oldest known prose work written in Latin. Different authors (Brehaud, 1933; Sáez 1996) indicate that the importance given by Cato to vines and olives reflects the transition from subsistence agriculture, based on cereals, towards a more commercial agriculture, in which wine and olives played a significant role.
>
> In his oeuvre, Cato explains the way vines should be married to trees, and how both should be pruned:
>
> *Be sure to begin in good time to prune vines trained on trees and to layer vines.*
>
> *Be sure to train vines upwards, as much as you can. The trees are to be pruned thus: the branches that you leave to be*

well separated; cut straight; do not leave too many. Vines should have good knots on each tree branch. Take great care not to 'precipitate' the vine and not to tie it too tight. Be sure that trees are well married, and that vines are planted in sufficient numbers: where appropriate, detach vines entirely from the tree, layer to the ground, and separate from the stock two years later.[10]

Although he did not indicate which species should be used, elms are cited many times in his book: they provide fodder for sheep and oxen (*De Agri Cultura* 5, 6, 17, 30 and 54) and how and where they can be transplanted is also indicated (*De Agri Cultura* 28 and 40). The second Roman reference to the cultivation of elms is found in Varro's *De Re Rustica*.

Marcus Terentius Varro (116 BC-27 BC) was Roman senator and led Pompeian forces in the Iberian Peninsula during the civil war. In his text, he considers elms the best trees for plantations because they are good props for vines, good fodder for cattle, they provide good poles for fences and firewood (Gil et al., 2003).

By the 1st century BC the cultivation of elms and vines together had become such a frequent part of the Italian landscape that the plant motif began to be used by Latin poets. Gaius Valerius Catullus (c. 84 BC-c. 54 BC), Roman writer contemporary of Varro, introduced the topic of the marriage of vines and elms to literature. Catullus identified vine and elm with wife and husband, respectively, in *Carmina* (Poem LXII: Nuptial Song By Youths And Damsels, verses 49–60; Burton and Smithers, 1894):

E'en as an unmated vine which born in field of the barest
Never upraises head nor breeds the mellowy grape-bunch,
But under weight prone-bowed that tender body a-bending
Makes she her root anon to touch her topmost of tendrils;
Tends her never a hind nor tends her ever a herdsman:
Yet if haply conjoined the same with elm as a husband,
Tends her many a hind and tends her many a herdsman:
Thus is the maid when whole, uncultured waxes she aged;
But when as union meet she wins her at ripest of seasons,
More to her spouse she is dear and less she's irk to her parents."
Hymen O Hymenaeus, Hymen here, O Hymenaeus!

The Latin poet and mime Publius Syrus also lived in the 1st century (c. 85–43 BC). Native of Syria (hence his name), he was brought as a slave to Italy, but soon he was freed and educated by his master. His mimes became well known in the provincial towns of Italy and at the games given by Caesar in 46 BC.

All that remains of his work is a collection of Sentences (*Sententiae*), a series of moral maxims. One of these sentences says *"Pirum, non ulmum accedas, si cupias pira"* (You should go to a pear-tree for pears, not to an elm; Nisard, 1903). This maxim is probably the origin of the Spanish expression *"No se le pueden pedir peras al olmo"* (You cannot ask the elm for pears) and the Portuguese *"Não pode o ulmeiro dar peras"* (The elm cannot give pears).

With the meaning of asking for something that is impossible, the Spanish expressions would appear seventeen centuries later in Cervantes' Don Quixote, when vines were rarely planted together with elms as we shall see. But why did Syrus compare a pear tree with an elm, a species that does not produce edible fruits, instead of with any fruit tree like an apple, a cherry or a plum tree? The reason is, in our opinion, the cultivation of elms with grapevines, more frequent than other fruit tree plantations because of the higher profit obtained from the wine. Thus, although not pears, for Syrus the elms did give a fruit: grapes.

It's brilliant, and it's simple.

If you take a walk through the woods you'll often see thick vines of various species making their way up high into the trees. Sometimes they're so high up that you can't tell what they are as there isn't a leaf in sight below the leaves of the trees. In the tropics we found multiple varieties of passionfruit growing wild this way and we just had to watch for the fruit to fall in order to reap no-work harvests.

Some vines—like grapes—wouldn't work this way as the fruit would be mostly inaccessible and would feed the birds instead of you, but there's no reason why you couldn't pollard trees to a reachable height and then use those trees as living trellises as the Etruscans did. Your yields might not match those of a modern trellised system, but the trellises would be free—and it's quite easy to start lots and lots of grapes from cuttings and plant them all over.

Two years ago I read a book on vertical gardening which covered all kinds of string trellises, and wooden frames and arbors and cattle panel hoops and fan-shaped metal supports for roses. It was good, but you could go broke building things to hold up your plants. Still, there are some high-producing vining plants that really do great on good trellises, so sometimes we will spend money on trellising materials.

The Crickmore Trellis

Two years ago I installed a "trellis to make you jealous," as it was called by Josh Sattin on his YouTube channel. An acquaintance sent me the video and I thought: hey, why not try it? Later, someone tipped me off that the idea was not original to Sattin, and that the same design was used in a video by farmer Connor Crickmore, released previous to Josh Sattin's video.

With that lead, I wrote Josh Sattin and did not get a response. I also wrote Neversink Farm. Connor Crickmore replied, "I have been using it for more than fifteen years," he wrote. "Like every tool, it is probably a combination of ideas, over time, and who knows where each aspect of it came from."

Good ideas often get repackaged and re-marketed as original or new, so this wasn't a surprise.

With this in mind, instead of continuing to call it the "trellis to make you jealous," we'll now just call it the Crickmore trellis. This design uses electrical conduit, PVC tee fittings and T-posts to made a sturdy and very long-lasting trellis that is easy to set up and simple to move.

We first built a Crickmore trellis to support tomatoes, then another for beans, and next thing we knew we'd built three

more long ones to trellis our true yams. The initial cost isn't cheap, especially at today's prices, but when you amortize the use you get from the system over years of gardening, it's well-worth the investment if you are a serious food producer. In the Caribbean, before discovering the Crickmore trellis, we used paracord strung between thick lengths of rebar hammered into the ground as a trellis, though that had a tendency to sag. It worked okay in the clay, but when we recreated it in Alabama sand it was not as stable. The T-posts and conduit idea was an upgrade and we have now abandoned my rebar and ropes system.

As each piece of galvanized pipe is 10' long, it's easy to calculate a row and fit it into a garden bed. 2 pieces is 20' of trellis, 5 is 50', 10 is 100'. I do recommend buying a T-post driver and a T-post puller if you decide to go with this system.

On the down side, these trellises are rather ugly and industrial looking, which I dislike. We've also built decent trellises from straight branches harvested from the woods. Take three long branches (7' or so) and arrange them into a tipi with the legs about 4' apart. Then build a second one about 8' away, and lash a long branch across the top connecting the two tipis. Put some strings down to the ground and you have a good trellis, which looks more like it came from The Shire and less like it came from a Brutalist architectural sourcebook. Branches don't last that long, but you can usually get a season or two from them and they cost nothing.

Cattle Panel Trellises

Another excellent trellising material that lasts almost forever are cattle panels. Cattle panels are super useful for homesteaders. You can make greenhouses with them, cover over a broken gate to prevent animals from escaping, make modular sheep-grazing pens, use them for the top of a grape arbor or even use them for a long-lasting fence around a small area. They're a bit pricey, but since they last, we keep reusing them for project after project. And as garden trellises, they are really hard to beat.

One of the best ways to use a cattle panel is to simply take an entire 16' length and bend it upwards to make an arch. Hammer two stakes into the ground where you want one side, then put one end against them and push the other end up until you're happy with the arch, then hammer in two more stakes, then zip-tie the stakes to the panel bottoms. We usually let the stakes stick about a foot out of the ground—rebar is perfect for this—with another 18" or so of stake in the ground. Each stake gets a couple of zip ties, and when you're done you have a very stable arch. These work really well to add more gardening area to a pair of beds, as the arch can go over the pathway and support beans, yams, bottle gourds, malabar spinach, cucumbers, loofahs, bitter gourd, cucuzza squash or even passionfruit. It looks good (though not quite Shire-worthy) when finished and covered with greenery and adds some more visual interest to the garden as well.

Another way we've used cattle panels is to cut 5–8' lengths of panel and set them up as vertical trellises zip-tied to a single T-post. Cut the panels in the middle of the squares with an angle grinder or bolt cutters so you have sharp protrusions sticking out on one side, then step them into the ground so those points stick into the soil next to a T-post in the dead center of the panel. This makes it much more stable and allows you to use a single post instead of the two that would be required if you cut the bottom end flush. Just those tines are enough to keep it from sliding around when a windy day pushes on the vines you grow.

We've also seen a cattle panel used as a good trellis via putting it long-ways across three T-posts hammered a foot into the ground. Instead of putting the panel flat on the ground beside the posts, zip-tie it about 16" off the ground, giving you more vertical space for the vines to climb.

This all assumes that you can afford and find cattle panels, of course. Down on the island we couldn't get them. There we often used an even simpler system, when we didn't want to bother with rebar and ropes. My friend James "Mike" Thomas would go into the woods and cut 8' lengths of hard, straight wood from wild coffee and other long-lasting trees and then hammer a single post into the ground for each plant. Two feet of stake was hammered into the ground, leaving 6' for the plants to grow on. We saw lots of pole beans and yams grown this way. It took a lot of work to do a big area, but farmers there had more time than money—and no T-posts or

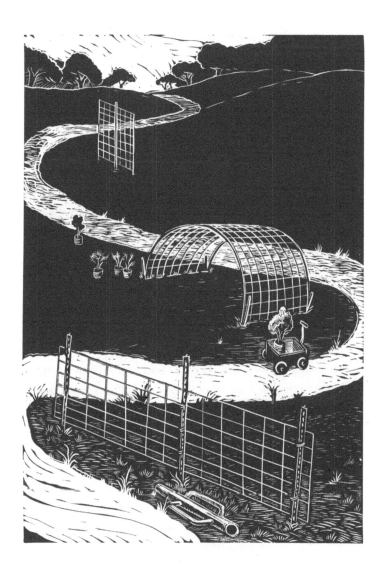

cattle panels—so they made do with what they could get. As a bonus, all the wood could simply be used as firewood when the bottoms rotted away.

Vertical Gardening the Permaculture Way

Another way to garden vertically is to do so without any trellises at all. You can use living trellises like the Romans, sacrificing less useful trees as supports for vines, but you can also just grow tall crops with progressively shorter crops on either side of them, with perhaps some vines mixed in, giving you more yield in a space and layering plants according to height, rather than building supports for a single species. This plays into the more long-lasting food forest idea of recreating a forest edge with a canopy, sub-canopy, vine, shrub, herb and ground cover layer.

One common method that uses a multilayered approach with annual crops is the famous Native American "Three Sisters" garden method, where you plant stations of tall grain corn on little hills, then plant pole beans after the corn gets tall enough, along with a ground cover layer of winter squash. We have planted this way multiple times but have not gotten the timing quite right or reaped decent yields.

Selecting the right bean, corn and squash varieties is important. When we tried it, we used a Grenadian open-pollinated corn variety just called "local corn," with Kentucky pole beans and a *C. moschata* tropical pumpkin with very vigorous growth. The beans weren't particularly happy and failed to yield much, and the squash liked to pull down the corn, so the combination wasn't quite right. Some experimentation is obviously in order. In a sense, we were cargo-culting a method that had been developed with specific corn, beans and squash in a climate far from where we attempted our Three Sisters patch. Getting the right combo is a job for a future gardening season.

Experimentation with recreating a food forest inspired vertical garden design in an annual garden has led us down some interesting paths. My current style of Grocery Row Gardening is working very, very well. Instead of just planting normal beds of crops in neat rows, we now mimic the layers of a food forest in our gardens, growing up rather than just out, with a big variety of annuals and perennials, herbs, trees, flowers and vines.

It is vertical gardening, in a sense, but without a need for trellises. We're capturing sunlight and water via the paths in between the beds and the up and down corrugation of plant heights within the beds.

If you consider each plant leaf as a solar collector, you can think of your garden as a huge solar panel array. Instead of being turned into electricity, your gardens are turning sunlight into sugars and starches. Some will be saved as roots, others as nutritious greens, others as fruits. The solar capturing capacity of a multi-tiered forest is far beyond that of a flat garden of green beans and the yields are higher as well.

Mike grew bananas and plantains with taro and sweet potatoes beneath them. Here and there he would plant a yam alongside a stake, also rising above the sweet potato ground cover.

Interlocking plants with different needs and heights can raise your garden higher and increase yields while also decreasing pest issues. Pests love monocultures but are confused when there is a multiplicity of plant species.

We've even noticed that leaving banks of weeds near our gardens lowers pest issues. Predators and other beneficial species need a place to live! When you grow "up" with multiple layers and a variety of plants, the fragility of your garden decreases.

Our Grocery Row Garden beds tend to be a three-tiered system, where we have a canopy layer (which would be a shrub or small tree layer in a traditional food forest), then a sub-canopy layer of berries, greens and taller herbs, then a groundcover layer that is often brassicas in the winter and sweet potatoes in the summer. Some of the ground cover layer overlaps in height with the shrub layer, like asparagus, taro and arrowroot, and some of the ground cover is perennial, like strawberries and creeping herbs such as mint and oregano. Despite the shade of the taller layers, the lower layers do great.

However, our sun levels here in the Deep South are much higher than they are farther north. If you have less sun, you might just grow a two-layered garden instead of trying for three. And if some of the layers overshadow the others too much, don't be afraid to cut and prune. As you do, drop the prunings on the ground for mulch, feeding the roots and the soil.

When a gap is opened up, plant something new in it. We regularly pop in seeds and transplants as we harvest and new spots become available. Adding in flowers and herbs is a great idea as they also attract pollinators.

Just remember: if you plant a bunch of one thing, it attracts plenty of pests. If you mix a bunch of plants together, especially if you have perennials and annuals together, you'll have less issues with pests and diseases. The perennials provide long-term hiding spaces for beneficial insects, frogs and other good guys. They also keep the soil alive by feeding the fungi and bacteria beneath the soil with exudates from their roots, meaning that anything you plant around them can benefit from living soil, rather than torn up, tilled soil.

Grab all the light you can, and grow up whenever possible!

And as a final note on trellises: when you're short on space, vertical is the way to grow. You can grow food in a 1' wide bed alongside the house if you run a trellis or strings up to the roof line. You can also prune and shape trees into two-dimensional fan shapes that will fit right alongside a fence or a wall. Don't waste time envying people with lots of square footage. Instead, think of how you can trellis and interplant and stack up your plants so they get the sunlight they need to keep your kitchen stocked with good food.

Cover Crops

When we moved to the Cursed Sand Pit of Death, as I like to call the house we rented after returning to the states in 2020, we discovered that our soil had a serious dearth of organic matter. To mitigate that lack, we planted a big mix of cover crops over more than a quarter of our roughly 10,000 square foot gardening area. The cover crop mix included mustard, turnips, daikons, cereal rye, pinto beans, black-eyed peas, winter peas, crimson cover and lentils.

The reason for the mix was to add organic matter to the soil and create a living polyculture to feed the soil biology. When you don't have enough compost, it makes sense to grow your own in place.

Some might say, "well then, just buy a few scoops of compost!" Yet buying compost has become difficult due to aminopyralids and other contaminants working their way through the supply chain.

The situation has evolved rapidly and nastily. Garden-destroying long-term herbicide contamination has now been found in hay, straw, manure, bagged manure from big box stores, potting soil mixes, purchased compost, mushroom compost and more. Sometimes you have to drive an hour or more to get hay that hasn't been contaminated with something. Around here, just about everyone is spraying—even the nice, innocent-looking Mennonites. It's insane.

It's so bad, it looks deliberate—and the situation is very complicated, since you have to think out any possible vector for the stuff.

Getting chicken manure? Wait—could the birds have been bedded in sprayed hay?

Getting cow manure from an owner who says he doesn't spray his pasture? What about hay—has he bought any during the winter that might have contaminated the manure?

If you get municipal compost, is it possible the pile had materials in it that were exposed to these toxins?

What a pain in the neck!

So, in the interest of getting organic matter in the soil without having to be on high alert all the time, we've experimented more with growing cover crops that will add humus to the soil and provide us with mulch.

When you have limited space to produce biomass, getting all the ingredients for a pile can be frustrating—but growing some cover crops is a nice way around the issue.

You can grow your own compost, right in place, with a green manure system – which is much easier than making a bunch of compost for your garden, especially if you have a large garden.

The problem with cover crops is killing them off at the right time to plant. We've done some experimentation with growing rye/red clover mixes, which we then sickle down in the garden beds and then plant right into. That works okay, but takes some effort. We've also done the same thing with black-eyed peas, which works well since they chop down fast and don't come back.

For improving larger areas, putting in a cover crop, then tilling it under and planting is a good method. Even better, plant a big crop, then when it's taller, scythe or mow it down and plant right into the roots and stalks, making a ready-made mulch bed. It's a bit hard to do but it holds back erosion and builds soil fast. It might be even better to grow a cover crop, then mob-graze it with cows to smash it down and manure the area, but that's hard to do on a backyard scale.

One benefit of growing and then cutting down a cover crop is that you can get two yields of organic material: the above ground leaves and stalks, which can be used for mulch or compost, and all the roots that are in the ground still, rotting away slowly and feeding the next crop. Poor soils greatly benefit from this, especially if you feed the cover crop as it grows.

We've seen this work on a backyard scale with running chickens in a tractor through an area, then planting the heavily manured and denuded patch with something else. This fall we did it with wheat and rye and got a beautifully thick patch we were able to use for garden mulch. Now that the grains are cut back, the sugarcane we planted underneath is springing up, happy in that manure and humus-filled soil.

Chop and drop is my normal method. However, I have also read a good bit on incorporating crops directly into the ground via tillage to rapidly build organic matter while holding nitrogen in the soil for the next crop. Tilling is very easy when you have a tractor, but it's a pain with hand tools. In Grenada, we only grew chop and drop crops for mulch, as tillage was very difficult to do. Lacking a tractor also keeps you from obsessively engaging in repeated tilth-destroying tillage. It's just too easy. I tend to believe that simply dropping crops on top of the ground to rot down as mulch is more natural than tilling it into the soil.

Grain rye has an amazing root system which gives you an abundance of humus in the ground, so it's at the top of my cover crop list. If you want, you can even let rye grow to maturity, then mow it and harvest the grain. The abundance of remaining straw can then be used as mulch or compost.

Yet tilling it under earlier when green – or mowing it and planting in the stubble – allows you to get your spring crops growing in a timely matter.

We have lots of options in our tool kits. One final thing to remember about cover crops is that their benefit goes beyond just the humus they can generate. Keeping living plants on the soil feeds soil organisms and keeps your land alive and full of good sugars sent down through the roots by sun-soaked plants. Bare, sunbaked ground is not good. The more you can keep life going through the year, the better.

Don't worry too much about getting the "right" cover crops, either. We've mixed all kinds of things together over the years, combining legumes and brassicas and buckwheat and grains and whatever else we found. Just remember that having something green on the ground—or a mulch—is better than bare, dead, ground.

There are many ways to grow cover crops, just as there are many ways to grow food. Keep it simple. Sometimes the simple solutions will come from spending time in nature, like seeing how grapes grow up tree trunks. Other times it will come from reading about the gardening experiences of others. And yet other times, it just comes from throwing various methods and ideas at your backyard garden and seeing what works and what doesn't.

Chapter 9

Gardening Without Money

When did gardening become a hobby?

Growing food used to be the common practice of most of humanity. Yet now, *Homo consumeris* is ascendant, and most of our food is grown or raised far away, out of sight and out of mind, via a vast and powerful network of corporations. And when we decide we'd like to take back some of our heritage and plant a garden, we rarely know how to do so without continuing to buy from the big corporations.

Consider this MD&A excerpt from SCOTTS MIRACLE-GRO CO., February 8th, 2023:

> Through our U.S. Consumer and Other segments, we are the leading manufacturer and marketer of branded consumer lawn and garden products in North America. Our products are marketed under some of the most recognized brand names in the industry. Our key consumer lawn and garden brands include Scotts® and Turf Builder® lawn fertilizer and Scotts® grass seed products; Miracle-Gro®

> soil, plant food and gardening products; Ortho® herbicide and pesticide products; and Tomcat® rodent control and animal repellent products. We also have a presence in similar branded consumer products in China. We are the exclusive agent of Monsanto for the marketing and distribution of certain of Monsanto's consumer Roundup® branded products within the United States and certain other specified countries. In addition, we have an equity interest in Bonnie Plants, LLC, a joint venture with AFC focused on planting, growing, developing, distributing, marketing and selling live plants.[11]

Did you catch that? Your potting soil, your turf fertilizer, your gardening soil, your garden fertilizer and your transplants could potentially all be purchased from the same gigantic corporation. If you use pesticides and herbicides, you can get those from SCOTTS as well.

Once you research the massive reach of some corporations, you can't un-see the truth. We are given a great illusion of choice, yet much of what we buy is really just different offerings by the same giant companies. Our politicians are also controlled by these entities, but I digress.

You don't need these companies. Our ancestors did not, and many of them ate much higher quality food and had better local seed selections than we do.

We've been turned into consuming zombies. Every problem requires us to buy something, because that's how we've been trained.

I include myself in this. Breaking free of that web isn't easy. Sometimes it makes sense to just "buy" a solution to a problem, like when your tomato seedlings die in a late frost and you go out to the store and buy a six-pack of transplants. It's convenient. I have done it.

But what if you didn't have that convenience? We may not always! Again: we spent four years living in the Caribbean, where imported goods were expensive and many items weren't even available. Cattle panels and T-posts were nowhere to be found. No one had a wood chipper for "Back to Eden" garden mulch. Books were few and far between. Yet many people grew their own food, and we got to see how gardening was done without complicated solutions and purchased items.

In this chapter we'll take a look at many of the expenses of gardening and provide some good old-fashioned "third-world" workarounds.

Seeds and Cuttings

Gardeners in Grenada always saved seeds from their gardens. Jars and baggies and envelopes of seeds were always put away for the next year, and if you lacked seeds, there was always someone with extra who was willing to share some of his stash.

We were given seeds for corn and for pumpkins, pigeon peas and Jamaican sorrel, pole beans and lettuce, as well as sweet potato slips, yam roots and cassava canes. In turn, we shared some of the varieties we had brought in from the states.

Plants produce way more seed than is needed for the next year, and sharing the increase could become part of our culture again. Also, saving your own seeds helps adapt varieties to your backyard and your climate. People are always asking me "where did you buy that" or "how can I get X," and many times my answer is that I was given the original seeds or cuttings. We have given away many, many plants, and we have also been given many, many plants!

You can do the same. Meet other gardeners and share seeds. Sure, I like buying seeds and looking through catalogs as much as any other gardener, but I don't doubt that in a pinch, if I were dropped on a new property with nothing, and no money, and needed to start growing food, I could simply go ask other gardeners in the neighborhood for seeds and they would gladly share.

Would you give seeds to a stranger who asked? I bet you would, and many other strangers would do the same for you. We've actually made great friends that way. A few years ago we gave one couple about six fruit trees as a gift, since we found out they had moved into our neighborhood. I'd propagated the trees myself, and they liked gardening, so I loaded them up. Later, he brought us some chickens, and moved a giant mulch pile with his tractor. Now we are good friends and see each other regularly.

Buying "solutions" has detached us from our fellow man, and we turn to far away corporate entities rather than our neighbors. Seed-saving was historically a community affair, with seeds being gifted and traded and bartered locally. It probably will become that again.

Now let's say you can't find any other gardeners to share seeds with. I don't know how that would be possible, but let's say it is. In that case, you could easily plant dry beans, roots, various herb seeds and even fruit seeds from the grocery store or local ethnic market and spend less than by buying seeds online. We've even planted an entire bed of potatoes via dumpster-diving behind an Aldi's and planting the potatoes we pulled out. It's not a matter of money sometimes, it's a matter of will and of ingenuity. You can problem-solve, and once you start thinking around the supply chain, it becomes second nature.

We already talked about saving seeds in Chapter 6. It's not hard. You can do it, and when you do, save extra and share them. Of course, if you need some money, there's nothing wrong with growing some seeds and plants and selling them. Just doing a garage sale with a bunch of plants can work well. If you push harder, you can also create a backyard nursery and get licensed so you can sell at events legally. This also gets you the ability to buy from giant wholesale nurseries and then turn around and re-sell what you buy.

When you know how to propagate plants, you sometimes only have to buy one rare plant, then you can duplicate it infinitely.

We used to have a coffee tree in a pot, growing in my North Florida yard. During the winter I kept it in a cheap greenhouse between barrels of water which kept the tree from freezing. Every year it would fruit and produce a few handfuls of coffee cherries. When it did, we would eat the cherries and save the "beans," washing them well, then planting them in flats of soil on top of an inexpensive heat mat in my office. During the winter they would germinate, then we would pot them up in the spring and let them grow for a bit before selling the potted seedlings at the farmer's market. The original coffee tree cost $30, which was expensive to us at the time! Yet over multiple years, that $30 multiplied into about $1000 in coffee tree seedling sales. That's a great return!

Learning plant propagation saves you immensely. You can literally take an hour sticking mulberry cuttings into trays, then pot them up later after they root, taking another hour or two, water them for a while until they get a couple feet tall, then go sell them, creating about $2000 in trees in less than a day's total work. I'm not kidding! It makes a lot of sense to learn to bypass the big corporations as much as possible.

Keep your eyes open, and think about how you can find or create a solution, rather than buy one.

Trellises

So, you don't have money for the cattle panel or t-post trellises we talked about in the last chapter? Never fear. CHEAPMAN is here!

We grew a lot of true yams and pole beans on sticks when we lived on the island. And not even sticks that were joined into trellises. Just sticks we cut from the wood with machetes and hammered into the ground as supports. Cut yourself a 7' pole, chop one end at an angle to sharpen it, then pound it into the ground with a convenient rock. Now you have a support! It's time consuming, but it's sustainable and biodegradable.

As for strings, I suppose you could use vines or something, but I have given in to crass consumerism and bought spools of hemp twine or cotton strings. Nylon is tougher; however, you can't simply pull down the entire netting and vines at the end of the year and throw it all in the compost pile.

Of course, if you just use thin sticks or bamboo instead of strings, you can also dodge that problem. After a year, they'll be half-rotten and you can toss them at the base of a tree to rot down the rest of the way and feed the soil.

The older I get, the more I find myself disgusted with plastic solutions. The idea of buying stuff and later throwing it away in a landfill just bugs me. Yeah, the natural materials may take more time to build with and break down faster, but they return to the soil, rather than becoming more garbage.

And speaking of garbage, I'm tired of people knocking bamboo. It's a gift from God, and it's one of the most useful plants known to man. Sure, there are types that will run all over the place if untended. Sure, some of them will poke holes in the bottom of your favorite kiddie pool. Sure, some of them will invite themselves to grow through the crack in your asphalt driveway.

But consider its many uses!

Bamboo can have edible shoots and usable timber. We built the sides of our henhouse out of split *Phyllostachys viridis* canes. We're also using them for trellises. A friend in Grenada built an entire greenhouse from *Bambusa vulgaris* canes he harvested along the river.

Right now I have some fresh bamboo shoots soaking in a pot on the stove. And we have other canes from a clumping variety being used as tomato stakes. Beyond that, we also cut bamboo in winter to feed our cows when the grass has died back. During the pandemic, we even made bamboo tobacco pipes and smoked homegrown tobacco in the tropical jungle during lockdown, as there was little else to do other than garden and worry about the end of the world.

We've broken up dried bamboo canes and used them to start fires, and as highly efficient rocket stove fuel for making coffee and cooking meals. (If you don't split them, they'll often violently explode in a fire as the internodes heat up and pop).

I have made privacy screens and propped up trees with bamboo canes, raked up bamboo leaves for mulch and compost, made a grape trellis from cold-hardy bamboo in Tennessee, made wind chimes, created drinking cups, made bamboo flutes (poorly), and even made sculpture from bamboo.

If you are cheap, you need bamboo. It's an all-around plant, great for many, many things. And not all of them are invasive.

We have *Phyllostachys viridis* in the front yard, which is a runner, but it only puts up new shoots for a month or so, then quits making shoots for the year. Many running types are like this. If you can keep it controlled for a short season, you're good. Still, I wouldn't plant it next to a neighbor's yard, or in a small space. The running bamboos have a reputation for a reason. Yet that very productivity makes them a great asset. If you're cutting 40 canes or so a year for gardening projects, you'll want something productive. We're planting more, so we always have ton. Right now we have about a fifth-acre grove of yellow bamboo, plus some green clumping bamboos which are smaller. If we can also add Japanese timber bamboo, some running black bamboo, some more clumpers of various sizes, plus the best eating types we can find, we might almost be satisfied with bamboo.

Yeah. I'm a plant hoarder. But I have lots of trellising materials. And you can too!

If bamboo is not an option, you can get an infinitely renewable source of straight poles via coppicing a few trees in your yard.

To coppice a tree, simply saw it to the ground while it's fully dormant in winter, before it wakes up in the spring. When it wakes up, it will rapidly push new growth, making multiple new shoots instead of its original trunk. In a year or more, depending on the size of poles and the rapidity of that species' growth, you'll have a ring of nice, straight poles. Cut them off during dormancy and you'll restart the process. That spring, the tree will make more shoots for you. Hazelnut and chestnut were both commonly used as coppice trees as they readily grow lots of new wood. Willows were used as well, but their wood is, well, willowy, so it was more often used for basket-making, rather than as pole wood. We're currently experimenting with oak and sweet gum coppices in our woods. In the past, we had good luck coppicing a red oak in the food forest, then cutting off the new branches every few years. If you're interested in learning way more than you ever wanted to know about coppicing, check out the book *Coppice Agroforestry* by Mark Krawczyk. It's inspiring.

Living Trellises

We covered the old Etruscan grape-and-tree growing method earlier, but grapes are by no means the only plant you can grow up into trees. Some years ago we pollarded a sweet gum sapling at about 7' in height and used it as a living trellis for three purple *D. alata* yam vines. We also grew a yam right up alongside a struggling dogwood tree and ignored it for a couple of years. When it died back at the end of the second season, we started digging to see how big the root had become. To our great satisfaction, it weighed in at 27 pounds! According to my calculations, that one tuber contained 14,220 calories, which could keep a man fed for 7 days. Seven days! And we didn't even have to build a trellis.

We also grew a lot of velvet beans up to the lower branches of a water oak in my North Florida food forest, where they happily made lots of beans and self-seeded for multiple years in a row.

We also planted about five yams at the base of a black cherry tree and watched them climb to over forty feet up into the canopy, where they happily unfurled huge leaves. We couldn't have grown a vegetable garden under that tree, but when we paired it with a crop that liked to climb we had a winning combination.

Down in the tropics, we also made a fence from *Gliricidia sepium* cuttings, jamming them into the ground at opposing 45-degree angles and lashing them together to make a living hedge with diamond-shaped gaps all through it. That kept out wandering livestock quite effectively. It was also beautiful, but the landlord didn't like it and tore it down after we moved.

Gliricidia sepium is too tropical to grow in most of the US, but you can make a similar hedge if you have moist ground and willow tree branches available. Just cut good-sized sticks and put the bottoms in the ground a little before they wake up from their winter dormancy.

The resulting fences can be quite beautiful and only get stronger as they grow. Then, if you like, you can also plant vining plants at their bases, adding another layer of beauty and production.

Land

And now, let's cover the biggest obstacle many of us face. I can't tell you how many people have written and said, "I would love to garden, but I just don't have any space."

Whether it's because of apartment living, a bad landlord who won't allow gardening, a transient situation, or a spouse that only wants grass—a lack of land is painful to someone with a green thumb or big green dreams!

We've been there. When we expatriated from the US to the island of Grenada, we were forced to rent in two different locations. The first one was a 2.5 acre cocoa farm with lots of fruit trees, bananas, some raised beds, nutmeg trees and more. It was beautiful, though parts of it were quite steep, and we could garden all we liked. Unfortunately, the internet connection was terrible and we had a lot of trouble trying to get work done online. we searched for land of our own, or for another place to rent in the country, without luck. After a year and a half, we moved to a decent-sized apartment in town where we had good internet. Yet then we had another problem: no space to garden, other than a balcony!

That was no good. Here I was, a garden writer and YouTuber, with a bunch of potted plants on a balcony and no place to put in a proper garden. Sure, I could keep my blog updated and do freelance work online, but where would I record gardening videos?

We started asking around, and were fortunate enough to get permission to garden on a 1/4 acre lot about two blocks from our second-story apartment. It was covered with thorny trees and brush, and a crumbling house, but there was dirt there. With much effort, we cleared a piece and planted gardens again.

Later, we also received permission to garden at Grace Lutheran Church, where we attended as a family. There we planted fruit trees and shrubs, cassava, chaya and more. Eventually we did manage to buy land and started planting in earnest. Then, a year later, we had to leave during the pandemic due to a bad agricultural minister who wouldn't work with us, as well as restrictions and mandates we weren't going to obey.

So we ended up renting again, this time in Lower Alabama. And we planted on borrowed land.

At the end of last year, we managed to buy land again—and we're on our own soil, growing food without worries about landlords or space. However, if we didn't own land, I am sure that right now I could call up our local pastor and ask for a little piece of land for a demonstration garden and it would happen. We could also talk to neighbors, local businesses, or people who own empty lots. There are opportunities everywhere.

Some people never even bother buying land. Instead, they garden across a network of houses in the city. Curtis Stone, the "Urban Farmer" did that successfully, as have many others, though it helps if you're an extrovert.

Where there is a will, there is a way.

Sometimes we make snap judgements, deciding that we "can't" do this or that. I can't tell you how many people have said, "Oh, I'm not a green thumb."

And that's it. And that poor gal will never try again, because maybe once when she was 12 she killed a potted ivy.

Certainly it isn't ideal for a prospective gardener to live in an apartment. You might look at pictures of beautiful little farms and country gardens and sigh about it—but don't use what you don't have as an excuse to do nothing. If you want it, work for it. Make something happen. Stop selling yourself short. You have 24 hours in a day. Use some of them to make something happen. Go talk to a neighbor. See if you can put a garden on the roof. Ask a local church or business for some space. Join a gardening group and see if anyone has land. Maybe there's a community garden in your area? Maybe there's an older person who would like help in his garden? Talk to family members and see if they have land you can borrow. Or, if you're really desperate, go guerrilla garden somewhere.

You don't need land of your own. I read a book last year by cattle rancher Greg Judy where he talks about the many pastures he's borrowed for raising cows and sheep.

Don't let your snap judgment be your only judgment. Back up and say, "do I want this? How can I make it happen?"

Reset your thinking and let necessity be the mother of invention.

Finally, if you're at the end of your rope, just tell God what you're looking for and see what He says.

Many times, we just don't want things bad enough, so we make excuses instead of doing something. Go do something.

Chapter 10

Year-Round Food

We've gotten accustomed to buying fruit and vegetables both in-season and out of season. Watermelons in February, apples in March, potatoes all year round, fresh spinach in December... these prodigies do not represent the way food grows on our own homesteads—or in nature!

If you are eating from your own garden—and hopefully from the neighboring fields and woods as well—you know there is a season to everything. Here in Lower Alabama and the Florida panhandle, the gardening season begins when we start planting potatoes in February, along with our brassicas, beets and carrots. In March we plant beans, and put out tomatoes and peppers while attempting to dodge the frosts. In April, we really have the all-clear on cold, and the tropical vegetables like cassava, okra, yard-long beans, yams and sweet potatoes start going in. Mulberries are already fruiting in the field, and there are an abundance of edible wild greens in the yard.

Early May is the season for foraging dewberries and harvesting smilax shoots from the woods. The mulberries are now done for the year, and the gladiolas are starting to bloom. The potatoes are just starting to come in from the garden but the cassava is just coming up. All the turnips finish this month, but the sweet potatoes are just getting planted. We're collecting seed from our patch of radishes and planting okra. In June we'll start getting early blueberries, and we'll have more cucumbers than we can harvest—though the collards are now surrounded by clouds of white cabbage moths. In July, we'll forage the main harvest of wild rabbiteye blueberries, and hopefully some chanterelle mushrooms as the rains really come in. July is also watermelon season, and we really start getting okra in abundance as the heat and rain kick in. Our pumpkins usually finish up in July as well. August is when the okra is really kicking—provided we kept them picked in July—and the sweet potato vines rule the garden. So do the weeds, and keeping their growth under control is almost impossible.

At this point of the summer, we're mostly done with the gardening season until fall. The tomatoes are a rotten mess now, and the cassava plants are as tall as we are. Our yam vines are consuming all the trellises and making bulbils for fall. At the end of August is sand pear season, and if we're lucky, we have buckets to harvest and process. We also make compost from the piles of grass clippings we get from the yard, mixed with cow manure from the pasture. In September, we try to get the weeds under control and keep picking whatever we find in the garden, while trying to get space ready for planting again.

At the end of September, it's time to start planting fall gardens. We can get in another round of beans and cucumbers, along with some peppers and tomatoes if we have transplants ready. In October, we plant brassicas again, and sometimes some onions and garlic, along with lots of cover crops for fall and winter: Winter rye grass, regular rye, clover, turnips, oats, peas, wheat and daikons.

In the cooler weather, we also get the weeds back under control and start making our gardens look pleasant again. In November, we harvest piles and piles of sweet potatoes, and start pulling some yams. In December, the cassava and all the rest of the yams come out of the garden, bringing us massive piles of roots we can eat through winter. Fall and winter are also when we get the bulk of fruit from our potted citrus and satsuma trees. In January we usually get our first frost, effectively ending the gardening season until February or so, when we plant potatoes again and start the whole season over.

If you just shop at your local grocery store, you'd have almost no idea that this was how a year of food production went. It also varies depending on where you live in the world. In the grocery store, some fruits are available year-round from the tropics, whereas others are seasonal in various places and then imported to your location from a variety of nations and farms.

When we lived in the tropics, there was a citrus season and a mango season, and a definite avocado season, but there were many other things that were available year-round, such as bananas and vegetables. Your gardening was hampered by the dry season unless you had irrigation, but nothing kept you from planting year-round if you had the water.

The shorter growing seasons as you head north led to much more of a dependence on animal foods and storable calories, such as grains and roots that could be cellared. In the tropics, fruit is falling out of the trees all the time; yet in a climate like Minnesota, you really don't have that luxury and would die if you didn't plan properly.

Your gardening should reflect the realities of your climate as much as possible in order to keep it simple. Grow what was historically grown in your area for survival, and branch out from there.

If you're planning out a minimalist garden, think about what you can be eating from the garden as long as possible without having to plan out elaborate frost protection and greenhouses. If you can grasp the ins and outs of your climate, you can plant and harvest with it, rather than against it. At the time I'm planting potatoes, states farther north are under snow. Yet if we lived further south, we would harvest potatoes at the time they're just starting to sprout up here.

Planting and eating with the seasons was our normal course of existence for most of human history.

It's like the hymn "Great is Thy Faithfulness":

> Summer and winter, and springtime and harvest,
> Sun, moon and stars in their courses above,

Join with all nature in manifold witness
To Thy great faithfulness, mercy and love.

Or as King Solomon wrote in Ecclesiastes:

To every thing there is a season, and a time to every purpose under the heaven:
A time to be born, and a time to die; a time to plant, and a time to pluck up that which is planted;
A time to kill, and a time to heal; a time to break down, and a time to build up;
A time to weep, and a time to laugh; a time to mourn, and a time to dance;
A time to cast away stones, and a time to gather stones together; a time to embrace, and a time to refrain from embracing;
A time to get, and a time to lose; a time to keep, and a time to cast away;
A time to rend, and a time to sew; a time to keep silence, and a time to speak;
A time to love, and a time to hate; a time of war, and a time of peace.

I grew up in a tropical climate and have had to learn patience with winter. By the end of the cold, I am itching to work in the garden again. As we get older, my wife and I have learned to appreciate the cold more, as the winter gives us time to clear brush and dead weeds away, plan new beds, buy seeds and work on non-garden projects, like organizing the homeschooling year, writing books, visiting family, sorting seeds, and doing indoor work like trying to reorganize my massive library (of which I would never brag about in a book).

Chapter 11

Putting it all Together

Remember, one of the main benefits of keeping your garden minimalist is that it becomes less fragile, or perhaps even antifragile, benefiting from disorder! You fertilize with what you have, you rely on good hand tools that keep you from relying on supply chains and gasoline, you learn the crops that grow in your climate so you aren't fighting nature and you avoid spending money on unnecessary things. If the lights go out, you are still able to grow food, just as people do across the globe under what we would consider exceedingly primitive situations.

The mindset is what's important. Learn to be your own boss in the garden and to make decisions quickly and learn from failure. Learn that buying products to solve problems is often not the correct response.

A lot of our gardens are not nearly as successful as they could be because we want to do everything by the book. A manager of multiple companies once shared something that really stuck with me. He told me that most people don't want to make decisions. They would rather someone else make the decisions. Sure, they'll grumble and complain about decisions that are made by their managers, but they wouldn't want to choose a path if they had the power. In effect, they're terrified to take hold of their own destiny.

If you make a decision, you are responsible for the results of that decision. You have to answer for it. If you're an employee somewhere in the middle of the hierarchy, there is a fear that a wrong decision will make you look bad, so you kick it up the chain to your supervisor and put him on the spot. If it's a big decision, he may then kick it farther up the chain to his boss. Eventually, it might reach the CEO before getting decided on. If he's tentative, it might get put before the Board of Directors. Very few people really want to make decisions for themselves. It's safer to pick a leader and just let him make the decisions for you.

That approach doesn't help you grow as a person. When we meet a born leader, we naturally gravitate to him because we're herd animals. Or we try to be very democratic. "Let's get a bunch of people together and we'll all ask opinions. We'll get everybody's opinion and we'll make a group decision."

There is an amusing Despair, Inc., poster that reads: "Meetings. None of us is as dumb as all of us."

Making decisions means that you are responsible, and sometimes that brings pain. Especially when we made a decision we were confident in and then blew it. I remember a man who threw himself into a business and failed, then spent the rest of his life living in regret. That one big failure wrecked him.

But when you fail, you should thank the Lord for it. Now you know what doesn't work. Get up, kid, and try again.

A good businessman might start multiple businesses that fail. Yet if you learn from each successive failure and get back on your feet, you are very likely to eventually find success. You don't need to ask for permission! Just go and fail grandly. Experiment wildly. Succeed magnificently. Just try crazy things for the joy of it.

I've done a lot of gardening experiments that didn't work. I once hacked holes in my front yard along the driveway and planted some corn without loosening the soil and without feeding it. I ended up with corn that was about six inches tall that made a couple of kernels here and there. It was the saddest looking corn ever. Yet I tried something similar with a different variety of corn, planted in the volcanic soil of the Caribbean and it did just fine.

You'll find people that are committed to their very favorite methods and evangelize for them constantly. Yet there are many different crops to grow, many different fertilizers that work, many ways to irrigate, many tools that you can use, many seed varieties, many ways to build a raised bed, and many, many methods across many cultures.

There is no universal gardening plan. There are basic principles, and then there are many pathways you can take depending on time, personal taste, climate, your level of organization or lack thereof, your rainfall, your energy, your goals... it just goes on and on. Don't get hung up.

If you talk to some of the hardcore biointensive gardeners, you'll think that double-digging, five-foot wide beds, tight hexagonal spacing and lots of compost crops are the answer. There are some excellent ideas there, for sure. That gardener might scoff at one of my wide row gardens or at your Back to Eden plot. Wide spacing and mulch are stupid!

Or another person might look down on your square foot garden. "Why would you bother with making a grid? I can't believe you're buying peat moss! Why don't you plant a food forest?"

You might love Paul Gautschi's Back to Eden gardening—it's no-till!—so you lecture your biointensive friend about leaving his soil uncovered. But Charles Dowding is also no-till but doesn't recommend permanent mulch because it brings in too many slugs in his climate.

So... what's right?

Build a garden that brings you joy and experiment all you like. If slugs are a problem, you might want to rake up your mulch and compost it. If you have terrible soil, you might want to make some raised beds with compost. If you don't want to irrigate, make a widely spaced single row garden. Or try every method that strikes your fancy.

You can also conduct experiments to see what works best by doing side-by-side plots.

We did that with soil amendments two years ago. And three years ago we also planted over a dozen varieties of tomatoes in the tropics in separate beds to see which ones would do great and which ones wouldn't. Out of all those, we found two that took the heat and the rain and the bugs: an indeterminate tomato named *Carbon* and a modern hybrid named *Heatmaster*.

One gardening season of experimentation was enough to give us answers to a problem that had been troubling us. Now we had two tomatoes that could be counted on. A few years later in Lower Alabama and we're also experimenting with two more varieties recommended by a some local gardeners: *Homestead* and *Amelia*.

You don't even need a big space to do some experimentation. Let's say you put four tomato transplants (of the same variety) in four pots. Fertilize one of them with seaweed fertilizer, another one with ashes, another one with diluted milk and leave one unfertilized as your control group and see what happens. Observe the results over the course of a season. You'll get a really good idea of what works and what doesn't. And when you shop for seeds, just buy dozens of different varieties and plant them one year to figure out what cultivars work the best for you.

You can short circuit this process a little bit by looking around your neighborhood for happy-looking gardens, and then meeting the owners and asking what they are growing and how they grow it. The successes and failures of others can teach us a lot and shave time off our own journey to success. Good books and videos can as well. Just remember that nothing can completely stand in for personal experiences.

If a particular plant was recommended to you, go ahead and try it. If it grows, great! If it dies, great! Either way, you have gathered more information.

Here's another way to think about it. A friend visited my garden earlier this week and was amazed by all the wild and abundant growth. "You don't spray anything, do you?" he asked.

"No," I replied. "I don't spray anything. I figure that if a plant dies, it's because it wasn't supposed to grow here."

We don't care about little holes in the leaves or the occasional abundance of aphids. Things happen, and we let them happen, and we re-plant plants that thrive, and don't replant varieties that are weak and wimpy. When you add seed-saving as a regular practice, you also start doubling-down on the tough plants. The strong, well-adapted survive. The weak do not.

We recorded a series of three videos teaching this idea of growing what wants to grow. The first video was titled "Comfrey is Terrible", the second video was titled "Comfrey is Amazing", and the third video was titled "Comfrey is So-So".

In the first video, I discussed how the herb comfrey is regularly recommended by permaculture gardeners as a vigorous and valuable nutrient accumulator and chop-and-drop plant—yet in our Florida gardens, it really didn't flourish like it did up north. We planted a lot of comfrey plants and had them die in the Florida heat. So, instead of comfrey, we started planting other fast-growing nutrient-accumulating plants such as *Tithonia diversifolia* and moringa to use in a similar fashion to the permaculturalists with their comfrey patches.

In the second video, I make the case for comfrey and share how useful it was when we lived farther north and it thrived.

In the third video, everything just falls to pieces and I sing a song about how ambivalent I am about comfrey, which really doesn't teach anyone anything but kept us amused.

The point of this entire series was to teach people to *think for themselves*.

One size does not fit all. You may have a particular plant species or cultivar that does amazing for you, whereas another gardener may completely fail with that plant. It might be related to soil, climate, gardening style, watering, care, genetics—who knows? But don't be afraid to gather information by planting a lot of different things and then letting the stupid pain-in-the-neck plants die.

We live in a choose-your-own-adventure world. There is a ton of information and treasure out there that we could just find. There are veins of gold in some hills and remarkable genetic combinations hidden in some plants. Nature responds to us. When plant and prune and weed and compost and save seeds, nature responds.

This is why we save seeds, experiment with creating connections between plants and animals and annuals and perennials, look for patterns and follow where they lead, and plant lots of fruit and nut tree seeds to see what interesting varieties might show up.

You don't know what you might find unless you give it a go. Sure, some apples might turn out sour, but you also might discover the next Granny Smith apple. Or at least, something interesting you can name and pass on to your children.

Conclusion

We'll conclude with a story of unexpected bounty.

Some years ago I read about a tree in India that made a "nut" that could be used as a substitute for soap. It's called the "soap nut tree," though it's actually the dried flesh of the tree's fruit which is used for soap. The Latin name is *Sapindus mukorossi*. According to some sites, it's fully tropical, and according to other sources it can grow into zone 8. Either way, I never saw one in the United States; however, I did discover that it had a cousin that was a Florida native. It's name is *Sapindus saponaria*. Hey—that would be great to grow, I thought.

Unfortunately, according to UF, it's only hard to USDA Zone 10, and at the time I wanted to grow this tree, I lived in North Florida on the border of 8 and 9. Yet on doing more research, I discovered that Chiappini Native Farm and Nursery in Hawthorne, Florida—which is in zone 8—had a large fruiting tree growing right out in the open.

I went and visited that tree, and was allowed to bring some seeds home with me.

So, who was I to believe regarding the cold-hardiness of the Florida soap nut tree? Should I trust the most prestigious agricultural college in the state... or should I trust Mr. and Mrs. Chiappini? As the latter were literally growing the tree, it was an easy decision.

So I planted my own, putting six of them in my yard. They grew wonderfully and quickly. Unfortunately, I read online that it takes about a decade for them to fruit when grown from seed.

Then permaculture guru Alex Ojeda from Jacksonville paid me a visit and said, "Oh, you have soap nut trees? I grew some of those from seed. They fruited in three years." Three years, not ten. And zone 8, not zone 10.

Sam Singleton, owner of the Scrubland Farmz Nursery in North Florida planted some of my seedlings and found the same to be true. Zone 8 was just fine—and they fruited in three years.

Do you get what I'm saying here? If you just believe everything you read and are discouraged from trying things for yourself, you will miss out.

If you have an idea, go ahead and try it. See what happens. Your fear is part of the junk you need to ditch. Life is short.

Experiment. Learn. Adjust. Plant exuberantly. Don't be afraid to be thought "crazy," and don't take the official advice too seriously.

And above all, cut the junk out of your life and your garden. You can do a lot more with less.

Notes

1. newscientist.com/letter/mg17723874-500

2. scribd.com/document/407789855/SRAC

3. youtube.com/watch?v=oifWngdzwCg

4. offthegridnews.com/alternative-health/the-toxic-truth-about-cinder-blocks-every-homesteader-should-know

5. extension.iastate.edu/smallfarms/toxicity-concerns-about-raised-bed-construction-materials

6. crops.extension.iastate.edu/encyclopedia/soil-erosion-agricultural-production-challenge

7. waldeneffect.org

8. waldeneffect.org/blog/Disadvantages_of_drip_irrigation/

9. guadoalmelo.it/en/wine-and-the-etruscan-ii-the-married-vine-three-thousand-and-more-years-of-viticulture-and-art/

10. *De Agri Cultura* 32; Dalby, 1998.

11. https://www.sec.gov/Archives/edgar/data/825542/000154638023000015/smg-20230401.htm

Made in United States
Cleveland, OH
11 July 2025